IT WAS NECESSARY COPYRIGHT © 2020 TURNING THE PAGE PUBLISHING LLC
All rights reserved. No portion of this book may be reproduced, scanned, or distributed in any form without written permission from the publisher, Turning The Page Publishing, LLC.
ISBN: 9798690622176

INTRODUCTION

I think we all can agree that we have come face to face with obstacles that we thought would take us out, literally, but then we survived… we lived. We did not understand why we had to go through what we went through, but then later God revealed its purpose.

IT WAS NECESSARY for our growth.

IT WAS NECESSARY for the development of our character.

IT WAS NECESSARY for the unveiling of our purpose.

Those things did not happen TO us; they happened FOR us. Because of those things, we are stronger, we are better, we are wiser.

The following stories are written by twenty-one other women and me; we have all endured real life challenges. We did not just endure, though. We overcame them. We allowed our trials to push us to triumph. The very things that were sent to break us, made us. The very things that were sent to take us out, brought us out.

It is our prayer that our stories encourage you and help you to believe that regardless of what you have seen or where you have been, God still has a purpose for your life. If you are in the midst of a storm at this very moment, know that you are not alone. God is with you, and He will never leave you nor forsake you. One day, you will look back and understand how this is aiding in making you who you were created to be.

ERICA D. BOYD

TABLE OF CONTENTS

FROM VICTIM TO VICTOR   1
ERICA BOYD

BEYOU: UNAPOLOGETICALLY   5
ANGELA LATREECE LACKEY

TURN UP THE VOLUME   12
TIFFANY K. GRIFFIN

DAMAGED GOODS ARE STILL...GOOD   17
CAMILLA POTTS

RESENTFUL TO RESILIENT   21
TOMEKA ALLEN

FROM THE PIT TO THE PALACE   27
ARLETHA ORR

MY JOURNEY TO MENTAL FREEDOM   32
DAVINA JACKSON

AFTER THE PAIN   39
PROMISE BRACKENS

THEN AND NOW   46
JEANETTE SEWELL

IT'S POSSIBLE   52
PEACHES SMITH

PERVERTED, YET CONVERTED BY GOD'S LOVE
HELL BOUND   57
ALICIA N. PERRY

MASK OFF, FINALLY SHERRY KINNER	64
GOOD GIRL APRIL WATSON	68
BETRAYED BUT NOT BROKEN ARIEALE MUNSON	74
IT DIDN'T BEAT ME JOCKQUELENE MITCHELL	78
JUST BREATHE JENNIFER WILDER	86
BREAK FREE........SPEAK OUT!!! MARISHA WALLACE	93
LOST BUT FOUND ESTEFANIA SUAREZ	99
DEPRESSION SPELLS I PRESSED ON FELICIA LITTLE	104
STILL STANDING JAMESE GREER	109
PAINED FOR A PURPOSE TASHIKA WILLIAMS	113
I PLANNED MY FUNERAL NATASHA R. KNOX	117
OUR PRAYER FOR YOU	122

FROM VICTIM TO VICTOR

Erica Boyd

I wore many labels growing up. I endured being called everything from a boy, to big-teeth, to an outcast. As far back as I can remember, I've had low self-esteem. This is due partly from things spoken to and over me to things that I spoke to myself. As a child, I can remember standing in the mirror picking myself apart and comparing myself to my counterparts. I used to think that if my teeth were smaller, if my hair was a little straighter, or if I was not so tall, I would be as pretty as my friends and classmates. I grew up in "the church" and I can remember my pastor always preaching that we were made in God's image. I used to think that if we were all made in God's image, then why were some of us ugly…like me. Early on, I learned to hate me and was convinced that God hated me as well, since He made me.

Because I carried these thoughts about myself, I was sure that everyone else carried these thoughts about me as well. This resulted in my search for acceptance early on, and this acceptance was often found in anyone who told me I was pretty, something that I desperately wanted to be. At the tender age of 12, being told I was pretty cost me my virginity, which opened the door to every kind of spiritual demon imaginable. It was not long before I realized that the 16 year old who took my innocence did not think I was pretty; but instead he used that to get what he wanted, and after he got what he wanted, he was on to the next little girl who had low self-esteem, too.

That hurt. That broke my heart. That changed me…FOREVER, and caused me to grow up fast, really fast. By the age of 16, I had been in and out of so many relationships. When one relationship failed, as they all seemed to do, I found myself in a new one. The same things that were making me sick became my cure. When that cure no longer worked for me, I turned to the life of lesbianism. I just wanted somewhere to belong and something to belong to, and at that moment, women met that longing for me. From there I went through a whirlwind of violence, drug use, alcohol, and anything else you can think of. I was so lost. It was not until I found myself in the emergency room having my stomach pumped from a drug overdose that God revealed His purpose for me. It was in that moment that I realized that God saved my life for a purpose. From that moment on, I saw myself differently. I no longer believed that my life was an accident.

As the adult that I am now, it's difficult to believe that I am the same person. It's difficult to believe that I did not die in the midst of my mess. It's difficult to believe that God uses me the way that He does. Today, the "same ugly big-teeth girl" who was looking for acceptance from anyone who was willing to offer it, the same little girl who hated her very existence is now a three-time author, a motivational speaker, a certified life-coach, and the CEO of a successful publishing company, Turning The Page Publishing…and it's all because of God's grace. I cannot take credit for any of it. God is indeed a promise-keeper and the master of making a mess a masterpiece.

If someone had told me that I would be this person as a child, I would not have believed it. No one could have convinced me of it. I literally resented God then because I believed that I was born to be picked on, mocked, and rejected..and then I would die. I did not see how I would ever be "good enough" for anything else…but then God changed the narrative.

My life is proof that we are all born with a purpose. The same things that caused me so much pain pushed me into my purpose. The very things I endured have enabled God to use me to reach others who have gone through or are going through similar situations, and because I overcame, I am able to speak into their circumstances and encourage them that they will as well.

IT WAS NECESSARY to have low self-esteem, to be excluded, to be rejected, to lose my innocence at such an early age, to venture into a life of homosexuality, drugs, and alcohol. IT WAS NECESSARY for me to attempt suicide. ALL OF IT HAD TO HAPPEN for me to become the Godly, transparent, bold, confident woman I am today.

STAY CONNECTED

Erica Boyd
www.ericadenise.com
www.turningthepagepublishing.com

beYOU: UNAPOLOGETICALLY

Angela Latreece Lackey

Ephesians 2:10 states, "For we are God's masterpiece. He has created us anew in Christ Jesus, so we can do the good things he planned for us long ago." If that notion is believed to be true, why is it that we lose ourselves in society's mock-up of what a man or woman should be? We work ourselves to the bone, just to be a size two or have a chiseled six-pack. We chase falsified popularity thinking that everyone will love us or hoping that they at least like us.

These were my goals at one point. I didn't fit in, so I disowned my identity. I was convinced that a chocolate, six-foot, lanky girl with glasses, horrible acne, and a size twelve shoe could never amount to anything meaningful. I mean, how could I? I was always teased for my appearance. Society had labeled me as "flawed."

In elementary school, I recall crying each day because I was teased, and sadly, if peers weren't teasing me, certain family members were. I felt like the black sheep of the family, so low self-esteem began to rule my existence at a young age. The events to follow only added fuel to the fire.

Early on, I was molested by an older cousin for several years. I didn't understand what was happening to me. People didn't have those important conversations with young children and adolescents. I don't remember anyone having a conversation with me to define appropriate and inappropriate interaction between opposite genders. Back then, people weren't so forthcoming about sex and other taboo topics. My molester told me that we were playing a game. So, whenever he saw me, we played the same game. Years later, I was able to put a name to what happened to me as a child. However, I never spoke a word to anyone because I thought I'd get in trouble. All the teasing and molestation contributed to my feelings of worthlessness and fear of ever being noticed again. I misunderstood the trauma to mean that something was wrong with me. I mean, why would he look at a child that way? Family is supposed to love and protect each other. It HAD to be my fault.

As I grew older, I began to compare myself to other people a lot, especially my siblings. They were very light skinned, had beautiful skin, could sing, and play all instruments – piano, guitar, and drums. They were awesome at sports. They always had money because they used their talents. On the other hand, there was me. I could only write and sing. I used to write my own speeches for special occasions at church and songs for youth revivals. I was smart – mostly an A and B student. The kind of smart that hardly ever had to study and was always bored in school. I didn't talk much. I hated being the center of attention. I tried sports and wasn't as good as I wanted to be, so I quit. In my mind, all I had was "book sense." Yet, despite being smart, many nights I cried myself to sleep wondering if anyone's perspective of me would ever change. Would I ever enjoy normal interactions? Would I always be teased? I prayed to God to just let me be able to sing well, to give me something I could use.

Living a regretful life in silence and feeling inadequate put me in a dark place. Once I started staying on campus at the local community college, I turned to alcohol, parties, and clubs. Every Wednesday, Thursday, Friday, and Saturday, I was at a party or at the club. At this point, I had even stopped going to church every Sunday. Hard to believe right? The "preacher's kid" skipping church, drinking, and clubbing. That was always the response I received once people found out who I was. See, I never partied in my hometown, but I knew every single hotspot in all the surrounding areas. While trusting the wrong people to shuttle me back & forth, I was raped. I never told anyone, until now – this very moment, at twenty-eight years of age. So, rewind a bit and add things up – always teased, molested several years by a family member, and now two rapes. Yes, two. They weren't violent with me, THANK GOD. However, they were both very traumatic. They drove for miles outside of the city and wouldn't take me to my dorm until I caved. I laid numb, eyes closed, crying, cringing, praying for it to stop. I must've stayed in the shower that whole night. I was disgusted. I buried it deep so no one would ever know. I was ashamed.

When I transferred to Jackson State University, I fell in love. In my first class, I met this weird guy. He wore humongous mud boots, dirty cargos, and a crispy clean white tee. He was beyond handsome and stood about six-foot three. I had a room on campus but practically moved in with him after a few months of school. He was the same age as me, but he was established. He was working for the Parks and Recreation division in his hometown. He had two cars, he could sing, write, and cook. He gave me all the attention I wanted, and he forced me to face the mirror. He noticed that I avoided facing myself. He broke a lot of the bad habits I had. He made me embrace myself – the way I looked in every moment. I was in Heaven, or so I thought.

After two years, he broke up with me because his girlfriend, who was enlisted in the Air Force, was preparing to come home for a few weeks. Girlfriend? So, most of the building he did to my self-esteem and self-worth slipped away. I would awake in the middle of the night, crying, and screaming. He practically ruined my senior year of college.

I got back with an ex after "Mr. Perfect" shredded my heart. I married my ex in July of 2014. I graduated from JSU in December of that same year, I decided to move back to my hometown in January of 2015. After we were married, I began to cry and scream in my dreams. He'd wake me from reoccurring dreams many nights. Finally, I told him about all the previous trauma, and he swore to help me heal. We had two beautiful children and separated after three years of marriage in August 2018, during our third pregnancy.

This broke me. All of the things that have happened in my life and now this? After I had confided in him about my ENTIRE past, I wanted to die. I tried to die. I would hardly eat. I couldn't sleep. I wasn't working, so I would take my kids to daycare and go home to drown in tears. I tried to flip my vehicle several times by running off the road, but nothing worked. I kept praying that God would fix me and fix us, but things got worse. Finally, I went to talk to someone and was asked a question. She asked, "I see that you're a good girl. You're grounded in God. You were fighting for him and his dreams and pushing him to the front…but who told you that your husband was the one in your relationship that was supposed to be out front?" (Hmph! Who did tell me that?) Then she asked me if he was fighting for me?

It wasn't until this time that I really bowed down to God and His will. Through Him, I started to come into my own. I changed my prayers to God. I asked Him to prepare me for what has to happen and to have His way in my life. I became more serious about my walk with Him, defining myself, and my purpose in Him – not a man or being a people pleaser. My prayer life blossomed. I began reading, studying, and writing. I learned to really depend on God. I've learned to trust in Him and not my circumstances. Now I know that only God's validation counts - not people's opinion. I was honest with God and told Him, "You're going to have to carry me because I can't muster up enough strength to crawl on my belly at this point." That's when God intervened. He began the mending and gave me the vision to propel others into total self-love.... beYOU Outreach.

If any part in this story has been you, it's okay because today closes that book and begins the culmination of a new story. In the Bible, Song of Songs (also Song of Solomon) 4:7 states, "For you are altogether beautiful my darling, there is no flaw in you." You mean - God calls me beautiful?! God...the Big Guy, Holy Jesus Christ - GOD! His word also says in 1 Peter 2:9, "But ye are a chosen generation, a royal priesthood, an holy nation, a peculiar people…". See human thoughts are not His thoughts! He chose me and You! YOU ARE ENOUGH!

So today…right now is The End! The end of brokenness. The end of self-hate. The end of dependency on man. The end of self-pity. The end of bitterness. The end of past hurts. The end of damage. The end of looking back. The end of fear. The end of bondage. God's word says, "Whom the son sets free, is free indeed…and where the spirit of the Lord is, there is Liberty." Well, the Holy Spirit is everywhere. He set you free through His Son on the cross. SO BE FREE! You are God's son or daughter, and you must embrace that. You're a kingdom kid. You're royalty. You're purposed for greatness. Rise up, wipe the tears. Adjust your crown. Simply beYOU: Unapologetically! I love you, but God loves you more.

STAY CONNECTED

Angela Lackey
jusbe1you@gmail.com

TURN UP THE VOLUME

Tiffany K. Griffin

There's a scripture in the Bible that says, "For I know the plans I have for you, declares the Lord. They are plans of good and not for disaster, to give you a FUTURE and HOPE."- Jeremiah 29:11

Some do not know the depths of those words. At one point in my own life, I'll admit that I did not know. My brokenness caused me to develop a deaf ear to what God was trying to say to my spirit. We hear things so loudly and clearly through the ears, but the voice on the inside is often turned down or we are consumed with things that keep us from giving our all to God . There is volume in surrendering all to God and opening ourselves up to hear Him clearly. For years, I have thrived off of the validation of man and what others thought of me. I had very little faith, and there was an overwhelming feeling of weakness on the inside of me. I could not fight though I tried with everything in me. I allowed others to dictate who they thought I should be. I was making choices that I was not comfortable with. I felt that a change would never come.

I 'd been misused as a child at such an early age. It happened to me for years. I knew it was wrong, but I thought I deserved to be treated that way. I thought I deserved to be molested, raped, physically beaten, emotionally abused, lied to, cheated on, etc. I felt that way because no one ever tried to instill anything different in me- no one except my sweet granny. God, rest her soul. Even she didn't know how to prepare me for the troubles of this world. I do know that she covered me in prayer. I do know that I am still living on grace and mercy through her prayers until this day.

My life had always been a rollercoaster with trying to fit in. I never knew how to be Tiffany. Surely, that was and is my name, but that was not who I was. I did not know how to be who I was- uniquely, wonderfully, beautifully, strongly, and proudly made in God's very own image. The long sufferings, rejections, betrayal, insecurities, judgements, loneliness, feeling unloved, being lied on and lied to, being disrespected, being talked about, feeling trapped, feeling unappreciated, feeling broken, and being bitter, angry, robbed me of me. I did not understand that God designed me in HIS image of perfection. He never said that I would not suffer or face obstacles that would cause me to stumble along the way. These things HAD TO HAPPEN for Him to get me to where He was taking me. All of those things have worked together for my good.

In order for any of us to get to where we are going in Him, we must allow Him to set us free. God is still, to this day, taking shackles off of me, and I am 46 years of age. I am just truly accepting, loving myself and realizing that He is greater than what is in this world. Molestation had me bound almost all of my life. Infidelity had me bound and insecurity nearly took me out. I did not like anything about myself. I thought others were better than me, looked better than me and were more deserving than me. I forgot to include, I've had two failed marriages. The only thing I ever wanted was to be accepted and loved for who I was, but then I came to the realization that no one would ever accept and love me if I didn't love myself, and if I didn't know who I was in Christ. None of my relationships would have ever survived for those reasons alone.

God revealed to me that if I wanted to live the life I was praying for, I had to turn up the volume on the inside of me. I could not hear His voice because I had a closed heart. I was connected to things and people who were not for me. It has taken me nearly my entire life to realize that I ALREADY have all I need on the inside to be who I have been called to be. My lack of trust in men also affected my trust in God, simply because I viewed Him as a male. If my very own earthly father did not sacrifice for me, how could I think that Jesus would? I had to begin to listen to and read God's Word as much as I could.

None of us will ever be free of hardships in this world. As soon as we accept that, we can truly live the life He has called us to live. The hardships are not meant to harm us; the hardships are meant to push us into the arms of Jesus. I am determined to speak His truth. I am determined to let all who hear me know I am where I am today because of my own decisions. I had the volume turned down. As soon as I turned up the volume, I started walking in some of the best days of my life.

God accepts us for us. He does not turn His back on us when we fail Him or disappoint Him. We, too, must learn to do the same. I had to learn that through all of my brokenness, He was there all of the time. I finally know who I am, only because I turned up the volume to listen to Him. I no longer listen to myself, my family, nor my violators.

Surrendering is all it takes. Turning up the volume does not mean that you will always hear Him clearly, but you will hear him if you sit long enough, open your heart and mind, and listen to him speak to you. God will validate you. In God, we are complete, and we lack nothing. He knew the troubles we would experience before we were born, but He also knew that He would be there with us through all those troubles.

Turn up the volume and know who you are in God!

Turn up the volume and let Him speak to you as it relates to your purpose!

Turn up the volume to receive His peace!

STAY CONNECTED

Tiffany K. Griffin
tkgriffin74@gmail.com

Camilla Potts

DEPRESSION almost killed me. SICKNESS filled me. BROKEN HEARTS confused me. FORNICATION used me. UNEMPLOYMENT found me. WRATH crowned me, BUT the GRACE of God saved me from the hands of Satan He raised me.

Before I truly sought God, I went through some things. I didn't understand the trouble my actions would bring. By having sex out of wedlock and just living in the world, I was thirty and single with three kids- 1 boy and 2 girls. I thought I knew what love was, but I was obviously clueless, trying to hold on to men I didn't need only made me feel useless. Not having full-time work added to my ongoing stress.

Looking at my babies daily, I felt as if I wasn't giving them the best. Living at home with my mom, my self-esteem started going under. Blood pressure through the roof; at any moment, I could've perished. I sat in a dark room, cried all the time. Regretted my last child and didn't fully accept that she was mine. Once a woman who felt beautiful with 2 college degrees, I was now in a whirlwind that brought me to my knees. What have I gotten myself into? Is it too late to get out? Do I really deserve all of this?

Time after time, God showed me things. He gave me revelations about unhealthy relationships in my dreams. As I ignored the signs, my life only got worse. As my heart shattered into pieces, I felt I was being cursed. From dreams to reality, God let me see with my eyes how the man I thought I loved wasn't really mine. My nights became longer, and the days grew shorter. I deeply regretted the moment I realized I was pregnant with my last daughter. With a heart set on ending her life before it could really begin, I quickly realized I was caught up in a life of sin. So much hurt, anger, and disappointment built up in me. I felt myself becoming someone I knew God didn't intend for me to be. I wanted to really hurt the man who was truly my enemy, but I knew no one could love and take care of my kids like their mommy.

As I watched my first daughter get in fire ants that quickly covered her little feet, I sat there motionless without attempting to get out of my seat. My body was very present, but my mind and soul had drifted away from the ones I loved most and the place I dreaded to stay. Once I came back to earth and realized what I had done, tears came flowing from the rising to the setting of the sun. I knew then I couldn't raise thriving children in the state I was in. I had to get out of the dark place I had been. I "knew" God, but I didn't know Him for who He could be, until I laid out on the altar for Him to work on me.

My prayers alone couldn't bring the change I needed. On my behalf, trusted family, friends, and church members interceded. Day by day, one prayer, one breath at a time, I started taking back this life of mine. I got rid of those things and people that meant me no good. I praised God and repented daily because I finally understood that I couldn't get through anything in this world alone. That's why my Heavenly Father sits on the throne.

As I look back, I know it was all meant to happen that way. I was being prepared for the better place I'm in today! 7 years later, I'm happily married with 5 kids and a dog, a great job, a nice home, a bed in which I sleep like a log, two nice cars, clothes, and food too! God has been so good to me, and He'll be just as good to you!

He gets all the glory. He deserves all the praise! I could've been lost, locked up, or sleeping in my grave, but God said no! He had a hope and future for me! He took me down to get to know Him and brought me back up in victory! He let me live to be a testimony for others. And I don't mind sharing my story with my dear sisters and brothers! UNCONDITIONAL LOVE has found me! PEACE surrounds me! JOY fills me! FAVOR thrills me! GRACE covers me! BLESSINGS pour over me! God has His hands on me! My present and future are better than my history!

STAY CONNECTED

Camilla Potts
author@camillapotts.com
camillapotts.com

My mom transitioned from Earth when I was 10. My dad had a family of his own although I was his first and oldest child. Due to me not having either parent in my life growing up, I became bitter & extremely resentful. I had a way of "masking" things to appear a certain way, but deep down inside, I bottled up emotions, suppressed anger, and most of all, I lacked drive to move forward.

    I was introduced to my God-parents shortly after my mom's death, and it was during that time I became somewhat hopeful. They reared me up in a Baptist church where I became acquainted with a lot of wonderful people who I remain in contact with to this day. I know "they" say, "Don't Question God," but I did. I wanted to know why God chose me to be motherless and fatherless. I found myself growing so cold and heartless, blanketing my emotions. Tears are falling as I type these words because the wounds are still fresh as if these things just happened. Being vulnerable and let-down have always been fears of mine. I showed no emotion at all.

    I was attending cosmetology school my sophomore year in high school and completed the course in April of 1994, a month before my high school graduation. I buried myself in work as a hairstylist for over twenty years to keep my mind off of things I had no control over and didn't realize it at the time. I had two young daughters by the age of twenty-one. My first child was born when I was nineteen. I struggled to raise them and take care of myself all while trying to figure out this thing called "life."

Everything I received in life was by trial and error. Everything I learned in my adulthood was by trial and error. I had no one to confide in who was trustworthy. I had no mentor, and during that time we didn't go to preachers or pastors for counseling. We figured it out day by day, and it seemed as if I was in this world, left to fend for myself and my kids alone.

I constantly questioned God. In January of 2003, I had a near death scare. I was experiencing excruciating pain in my chest, and it was uncontrollable. Although the pain had started three months prior, it had gotten so bad I couldn't lay down at all; it was unbearable. I had to sit in a recliner for two weeks just to sleep. The pain finally forced me to go to the emergency room.

Once there, the nurses rushed me to the back on a stretcher and gave me all kinds of pain meds, but it didn't stop the pain. After many attempts to resolve the pain, I finally passed out because I couldn't bear it anymore.

My body wasn't responding to any of the medication, yet I was still able to hear conversations around me. I heard the doctor tell my cousin that I had an enlarged heart and there was nothing else they could do. Everyone burst into tears. All I could do was lay there and think about my kids and once again, question God. I asked God, "Don't you think I've been through enough pain already?" He said, "Trust the Process." I passed out again, but this time when I awoke, I was at the University of Medicine in Jackson, MS.

Once I regained consciousness, I was given something for pain and that was the first sign of relief I had felt in three months.

I had to have surgery to have a bronchiole cyst removed that had been developing since birth, and I had no knowledge of it. When I regained consciousness from surgery, I was told by the operating physician that he had good news and bad news. I whispered as best as I could to him and said,"Just tell me and get it over with."

He said, "The good news is we were able to remove the cyst, but we also had to remove a portion of your lung because the cysts had grown attached to it, and it was the size of a coconut."

He also assured me that I would be just fine.

My dad came down and stayed a week with me in the hospital during my two-month stay. Three days later, I began to feel another form of excruciating pain similar to the pain I experienced when I was rushed to the emergency room. Here I was, thinking I was on my way to recovery only to find out I had to have an emergency surgery to remove the remainder of my lung.

AGAIN, I questioned God. "How much more pain are you going to put me through?"

It was at that moment that I became more and more resentful. Living in a state of resentment had become my norm.

After surviving that painful but necessary ordeal, I had yet another scare. I had been married for five years at this point. My husband and I were in the middle of a very "rocky" time in our marriage. I stepped outside our marriage for my own personal reasons, and we almost didn't make it. Again, that was another layer of resentment added. I asked God again, "Why? Why am I continuously experiencing pain? Why can't You just keep your arms around me? Everybody else is gone! What did I do to deserve so much without no one to lean on?" AlthoughI knew I loved my kids and I knew I loved my husband, I didn't know HOW to love.

It took my husband and I three years to get to a place where we felt comfortable around one another again.

I tried pushing him away because I felt like everybody was leaving or had left my life. I often wondered why he even stuck around. I asked God what my purpose in life was; I pleaded with God to show me what my calling was. I knew what my gift was, but my calling seemed to be totally different. That was in 2011, but He didn't reveal the answer to me until 2018.

See, God reveals things in His timing. He wants to make sure we're ready and capable to take on the tasks He has in store for us. God allowed me to birth ALL of that pain in order for me to understand my calling in life.

See, I made a lot of mistakes, but God showed me that EVERYTHING I went through, everything I endured along the way was absolutely necessary for my calling in life.

One of my favorite quotes states, "Mistakes are hidden lessons. It's up to me to recognize those lessons." Though I did not understand it then, the absence from my parents molded and groomed me.

After experiencing so much pain which built up so much resentment and so many layers of resentment, I learned a valuable lesson. God wasn't allowing things to happen TO ME, He was allowing things to happen FOR ME.

I pray and hope this blesses someone's spirit because if God did it for me, He can and will do it for you.

God transformed me from Resentment to Resilience.

STAY CONNECTED

Tomeka Allen
mizallen1105@gmail.com

All'En
Life Coaching

May you continue to be prosperous & blessed ♡

Tomeka Allen

FROM THE PIT TO THE PALACE

Arletha Orr

Oftentimes in life, we as women neglect ourselves to take care of others around us. We put our dreams and goals on hold to help others achieve theirs-significant others, children, family, friends, etc. By the time we've helped everyone else, we're too exhausted to do what we have been called to do. We're tired and burnt out from being the wife, mom, teacher, caregiver, lover, friend, therapist, and nurse. When do we accomplish what we want to do in life? When do we revisit our dreams and goals and live for us?

If you are a woman, I'm pretty sure you have felt that way at least once in your life. Most of the time we do forget ourselves and focus on others, but here's the killing part- we never notice it until years have passed, and then we find that it's too late.

In July of 2008, I gave birth to my first child. She was my world. I was a single parent, so we spent a lot of time together. Immediately, I started to instill morals and values that would prepare her for life. I made sure she started school at the appropriate age so that she could start learning to be interactive with other kids, learn motor skills and more. She knew how to behave at church and even at restaurants. I'll never forget it; I received an acceptance letter for nursing school. I started, but then decided to quit because I couldn't focus like I needed to. I wanted to make sure my daughter did not lack anything, so I withdrew from nursing school and chose something a little less complicated that didn't require so much of my time.

For five years, it was just the two of us. In May of 2012, I met my husband and in May of 2013, we were married. It was a joy to have him as a father figure in my baby's life and also to have a man around the house. During this time, he taught our daughter how to ride her bike and rake leaves. He also assisted with homework and so much more. We were both "happy as hyenas."

In December of 2014, God blessed us with an addition to our family, a baby boy. We were all excited! It was my husband's first son, and my daughter enjoyed the adventure of being a big sister. They loved each other. They were both enrolled in school and doing great. We attended church as a family. We went on vacations and did everything a family is supposed to do. Life was perfect! The absolute best eight years of my life!

In May of 2016, I lost it all. My hubby picked up the babies from after-school care, and as they were traveling home, they were struck by an Amtrak train. Neither of them survived. I had recently spoken with my husband an hour before the accident occurred. It's amazing how one day everything can be perfect, but within the next second, it all vanishes. That day was no different than any other day. It was a normal drop-off work and school day, but that evening changed my life.

During this time, unknowingly to me, I had lost or hidden some things that made me happy. Of course our goal as a mom and wife is to make sure everyone is taken care of in the house, but we neglect ourselves. Please don't misunderstand. Being a wife and mom were the BEST things that ever happened to me in my life. However, we should never forget or lose focus on ourselves.

A pit is a hole that serves as a trap! When you're in a pit, it's dark and gloomy and you can't see your way out. The worst part about it is sometimes we don't know we're there because it has become our norm. We're broken, hurt, and don't have the capacity in our hearts to forgive. It's our comfort zone and we're okay being there. When we look at a palace, we think of a royal place. People are happy, dancing, eating and enjoying life. Who wouldn't want to be in a palace or have a palace experience because it seems magical?

After the accident, I was devastated. I was literally in a pit because I felt as if I had nothing. I felt isolated and hurt. My family was my everything. I loved being a mom and a wife. In the midst of me crying and throwing a pity party, God gave me a word. He spoke "LIVE!" That didn't quite register with me at the time because I was alive. I asked God, "What do I do? Where do I go from here? What does that mean?" He spoke again and said, "LIVE!" I said, "Okay God."

I have been alone for four years now. I have learned, and I am still learning what He meant by "LIVE.". During this time, God has revealed a lot to me. He has restored my joy! He has restored my peace! He has given me the courage to face things that I swept under the rug. He has revealed so much about me, and I thank Him for it. God needed to renew my mind. I can't step into my "newness of life," also known as the palace, with a pit mentality.

Now, I see myself in the palace because I'm free!!! Somewhere along the way, I forgot what made Vonda happy. I put everyone else's feelings, needs and desires, before my own. When God spoke, I began to travel more, laugh more, and take myself on dates. I began to LIVE!

I want to encourage you to come out of the pit and come to the palace. Whatever has you bound, let God free you from it so that you can be restored! Let God restore your joy! Let God restore your peace! Let God restore your mind. Sis and Bro, you look so much better when you smile! No longer will you be bound by people or things. No longer will you be unhappy. You deserve to accomplish what you want in life! You deserve everything you desire to have!

Rise up Queen and King! Take what's rightfully yours. You got this! You are more than a conqueror! You shall LIVE and not die, and declare the works of the Lord! LIVE!

STAY CONNECTED

Arletha Orr
www.arlethaorr.com

I magine holding in your distress and pain for years, walking around with a fake smile on your face, but literally on the verge of breaking down at any time. Can you visualize carrying trauma, low self-esteem, and depression around with you from the age of seven to twenty-six years old? That's almost twenty years of torture, agonizing, internal torture. That person bearing all of that weight from her past, for so many years, was me. For nearly two decades, I battled mentally, trying to figure out who and what I am. I attempted to find my way through this world, find love, longing for understanding, for guidance and help.

My mental health issues were birthed when I was only seven years old. Mental illness does not care who it attaches itself to. You can be young, old, rich or poor. IT DOES NOT DISCRIMINATE. At this pure age, I was molested by a young lady whom I trusted, and she was a close family friend. Three or four years later, at the age of ten, I was molested yet again by a young man who was also close to my family. I will never forget those horrific incidents. I can recall the scent and taste of the female abuser; even now I gag at the thought of it. I can also remember lying on the male abuser's bed while being fondled and thinking, "I must really be special, everyone loves touching me, men and women." These horrendous incidents developed a ton of emotions inside of my tiny body and mind. Insecurity, low self-esteem, anxiety, depression, and so much more, and it only worsened as I got older. Do I like boys or girls, or do I like both? Is God mad at me for my thoughts and actions? There were so many questions going through my head, and so many feelings circulating in my body. I was extremely confused.

My abusers satisfied their twisted fetishes and went on with their lives like nothing ever happened, leaving me damaged. I felt like a nobody, and I also felt used. This left me searching for love and validation from others by giving a piece of myself to anyone who I thought cared for me. At fourteen, I lost my virginity to my then boyfriend, and we broke up a week later. My heart was unquestionably crushed because I gave this person something so special and he just took it and ran with it. I pushed my emotions to the back of my mind and moved on to the next guy and then the next, being let down every time. EVERYBODY who loved me, or so I thought, was the same- users and abusers. I was still that hurt and lonely little girl trapped in a teen's body.

I would often sit and think to myself, "Nobody loves you Vina, not even yourself. You're constantly giving your body to people thinking that they really love you when they don't. You're ugly and God isn't pleased with your actions. You should go ahead and end your life. Nobody will miss you anyway." I became violent towards myself and others. I began smoking, skipping/failing school, clubbing, and I slowly started to isolate myself from the outside world. Suicidal thoughts took over my mind causing me to write good-bye letters to my mom, and I eventually slit my wrist. One particular night, I was fed up with life. I just wanted to disappear. I locked myself in the bathroom and cried, looking in the mirror watching myself cry until my eyes were bloodshot red. I no longer wanted to be on this earth. I felt that no one loved me anyway. I lacked love and affection growing up as a child, and I was so desperately searching for it, but I had no luck. I felt all alone in this chaotic world. No one to express myself to coupled with no guidance and no understanding. I looked in the medicine cabinet and grabbed the first thing that I saw. An eyebrow archer. I took one last look in the mirror, raised the blade and slit my wrist three times, rapidly. In shock, I watched my arm bleed. This was it. I was ready. I ran a hot bath, undressed and climbed into the tub. I allowed my arm to hang outside the tub to bleed out, I laid my head back and closed my eyes preparing to die. I was 16 years old. After being in the tub for about an hour, surprisingly, I was still alive.

    I met my now ex-husband at the age of seventeen, and we married at the age of twenty-one. My mother begged me not to get married. Maybe she saw something that I didn't see at the time, but we tied the knot anyway. I wanted to be loved, and he claimed that he loved me. He asked me to marry him, and I of course said yes. I was happy and in love, so I thought. We had some happy moments, but we also had many not so happy moments. I went through a lot behind closed doors just to keep my marriage together, but neither of us were not mentally stable nor were we ready for a lifetime commitment. We both needed to work on ourselves before dating and getting married. It was a disaster from the start. At the age of 26, I separated from my husband. To my surprise, he was having an affair for months, with a girl that I knew, and I had absolutely no clue. Everyone knew my marriage was failing, but I was the last one to find out. At the time of the separation, my son and I were living with my mother. I had no other place to go, no money, no transportation, no one to talk to or trust, and depending on

God was definitely out of the equation. I was even more upset with God for allowing me to go through this. I began popping pills to help me sleep and drinking heavily. I would find myself drifting off to sleep swiftly when I was intoxicated, on the phone, driving and even in the bathtub. I was in a very dark place and I didn't care about anything. I was so irate that I began to lash out toward those who were there for me and truly loved me. I do believe that I was on the verge of losing my mind.

One particular day, I was sitting and thinking about everything that my ex-husband had put me through- the hurt, the embarrassment, the mistreatment and dishonesty. I cried, laughed, and cried some more. Then suddenly, I stopped in the midst of me crying and said, "I'm going to kill him." I drove my mother's car to the place I knew my spouse was living. It was almost one o'clock in the morning. My mom and my son were asleep so that was the perfect opportunity to get out of the house. I pulled up to the lady's house who was with my husband, put the car in park, sat there and just stared. I didn't have any thoughts at all; my mind was completely blank. I snapped out of my daze, took out my phone and texted someone I trusted and told them what I was about to do and asked them to look after my son. I turned the lights off on the car and decided to keep the car running because I figured I'd do what I came to do, jump back in the car and go! As soon as I reached for the car door to open it, my phone vibrated. It was the person I texted responding back to me. They begged me to go home and be with my son because he needed me the most. I stared at the text for a few seconds, and then looked back at the house. I drove back to my mom's house in complete silence- no radio, no tears-just a blank stare and a blank mind. The drive seemed very long to me, but as I drove home I realized that I was not who I wanted to be when I looked in the mirror. I was on the verge of losing it all and that's not what I wanted. I was tired of fighting the same demons over and over. For years, I had been in an emotional battle with MYSELF. I wanted a change in my life, and I needed that change fast before it was too late.

    After divorcing at the age of 27, I began thinking about me and my happiness. I sought professional help by going to counseling to guide me through my healing process. I developed a closer relationship with God to help me spiritually, and I began exercising, eating healthier and doing yoga to help me physically. I isolated myself from things that I figured would distract me from healing. During this isolation season I gained a best friend, who I now call my boyfriend. I didn't treat him too kindly in the beginning, but through all of my ups and downs, spazzing out, counseling sessions, doctors' visits, court dates and more, he has been by my side.. He has taught me the true meaning of love, patience, kindness and how to trust God through it all. He encourages me to follow my dreams no matter how big they are and motivates me to be the person I've always wanted to be-ME! I'm able to be myself, tell stupid jokes, laugh loudly, dance awkwardly, wear what I want to wear and do as I please. He's beyond sweet, loves my son to life, and God is the center of his life! He's my best friend and he has changed my mind about love because I didn't believe in it anymore. I'm not only a believer in love; I'm a believer in being LOVED CORRECTLY.

    So much healing has taken place and many goals have been made in the last four years of my life, and I couldn't be prouder of myself. I made one of the biggest decisions of my life four years ago and that was to remain celibate until I married again. I've gotten to know who I truly am, what I like and dislike. No one has control over my body but me! No more violating me, no more giving myself to anyone who "claims" they love me, and no more soul ties! I made this decision for ME and no one else, and anyone who does not like it, can remove themselves from my life. Celibacy is a form of self-love and respect, and it's my choice to practice. It's not an easy journey, but it is mentally and spiritually rewarding.

I've been living my best life since I chose to live a life full of laughter and love. I can look back over my life and see how far God has brought me. I've gotten my confidence back. I've learned to love who I am, and I've learned to love again even when I was afraid to do so. I've forgiven those who've wronged me and bitterness does not live in my heart. Mental break downs, suicide or divorce could not take me out. My past was traumatic, but my future is triumphant. I choose to continue my story, my testimony, and my life. I chose and still choose to LIVE. There's more to come after this.

STAY CONNECTED

Davina Jackson
jonnaejackson@gmail.com
Instagram: jonnaemakeup
Facebook: Davina Jon'nae

AFTER THE PAIN

Promise Brackens

One of my all time favorite blues songs is, "After the Pain" by the late, Betty Wright. I can relate to this song in so many different areas of my life.

I grew up as a PK (Preacher's Kid), and my life was great, or at least that's the way it appeared to be to others from the outside looking in. While I grew up in a two-parent household, had nice things, lived in a fairly decent neighborhood, I remember so many dark days where I felt abandoned and neglected, days where I'd cry all day, days where I just wished God would take my life. I remember days of being afraid to even be at home. Don't get me wrong. There were good days, but there were also days where there were lots of drama, domestic abuse, arguing, and so much dysfunction. I would often have friends tell me, "I wish I lived your life." The whole time, I'm wishing to have another life. They saw the trips that we were taking every summer, not knowing that we were only taking them because it was for church. They saw us staying in the nice hotels, not knowing that we had noodles, Vienna sausages, and sandwich meat packed, because we couldn't afford to eat out when we were out of town. Be careful of what you ask for. Everything isn't always as pretty as it appears to be!

I'm the oldest of my mother's five children, and I'm the only child with a different father. My mom's ex-husband is the only dad I knew. My biological dad passed when I was maybe two years old. Although my mother's ex-husband treated me like one of his own during their marriage, I still longed for my own father. I wanted that father/daughter relationship with my biological father. I was jealous of other girls who had their dad and had the opportunity to be a daddy's girl, and I felt less than others who were blessed to have their dad in their lives. Although my dad is deceased, I grew up being angry with him for not being there to love me, to have my back, and to protect me. I felt that if he had been alive, my life would be somewhat different, and I wouldn't have endured so much heartache and pain.

Around the age of 13, I remember coming home from school one day. I got off the school bus just as happy as can be. As soon as I walked into the house, my attitude and mood immediately changed from being jolly to becoming so furious. I was upset that MY mother was interacting with my step brother at the time. I was livid, HOT AS FISH GREASE! I stormed into my room and slammed the door to get my mom's attention, and trust me, I got it too. She yelled, "You don't pay any bills in this house to be slamming any doors. What's your problem?" The tears began to flow. After so many years of being molested, I finally had the opportunity to let my mom know what had been done to me without feeling embarrassed or ashamed. At that moment, I felt relieved, relieved that I didn't have to be afraid of being around him alone anymore, relieved because I felt like he wouldn't be able to hurt me again. Boy, was I wrong! After telling my mom what had been going on, she informed her husband at the time. Once he made it home from work, we discussed the issue, my step brother cried and apologized and that was it. I thought, "What a waste! I should have just stayed quiet about it."

That issue was kept inside of our household until I was old enough to publicly speak about it and not be ashamed of what other people would think of me. For a long time, I hated my step-brother. I didn't want to be around him at all. While I felt nothing was done to bring me justice, I played the victim and didn't do anything to heal. Instead, I became curious, and I felt like I was grown and ready to experiment with sex.

During my 9th grade year in high school, I met this guy who was about four years older than me. He was so affectionate, bought me gifts, showed me off to his friends, and reassured me that I was the prettiest girl in the world to him. Because I didn't grow up in an affectionate household, this was major for me- someone telling me that I'm pretty and not calling me fat, ugly, or funny looking. I was in love, or at least I thought it was love. After several months of talking, I lost my virginity. I gave in because I wanted to keep him around. He made me feel loved, he made me feel wanted, and he made me feel good about myself. Three months after losing my virginity, I caught him with another female. I was hurt, disappointed, and the void that I was trying to fill was a lot worse now.

During my 11th grade year in high school, my mom and her husband got a divorce. At this point I was convinced that God wasn't real, and if He was real, He didn't care about me. After the divorce, my step-father would come to get my siblings on the weekends. I knew that he wasn't my biological dad, but I started to question if he really loved me while he and my mom were married, or if he just tolerated me. I felt abandoned. Instead of me starting my healing process, I found other things and people to help me fill those voids. I wanted nothing to do with the church or God. I had this attitude up until I was about 21 years of age. I encountered toxic relationship after toxic relationship. Instead of dealing with my issues, my insecurities, and the wounds, I used temporary bandages, things, and people to cover them. Not realizing I was making the wounds deeper.

    I started dealing with a married man. Did I know better? Yes! Did I care? Absolutely not! This "situationship" lasted extremely longer than it should have. During this time I was arrested multiple times- in and out of jail for kicking in doors and fighting, being very manipulative, and out of money for court fines that I couldn't pay. I was angry, bitter, miserable, and evil. I was not only causing myself pain, but also causing pain to the people who genuinely loved me and wanted better for me. This may have been one of the darkest chapters of my life. My mom washed her hands with me, and if I can be quite honest, I didn't care. It had gotten so bad that my mom and I would go months without speaking to each other, and when we did speak we only exchanged harsh words. I promised myself that I would not call her for anything.

    I ate my words real quickly.

    By 2014, I was living extremely recklessly. Daily, I was partying, having meaningless sex, drinking alcohol, being a con-artist, playing victim in storms that I created, and the list goes on. I guess since I wouldn't sit down, God put a stop to my plans and forced me to sit down. I lost my job, became homeless, broke, sleeping on friends' couches and floors, going without eating some days, and I blamed God for my life being a hot mess. I had created this image that my life was perfect, so I couldn't be honest with anyone. I wanted to cry out for help but didn't want people to know the truth. After running from God so long, I cried out to Him. I literally prayed and cried for months for God to help me heal. Things eventually started to fall into place, and my mom was one of the people who helped me get back on track. This also allowed us to work on and mend our relationship. I now understand that the way I wanted my mom to love me, she couldn't give me that because she had no one to give it to her. Now, we communicate so much better, and she's literally my best friend. We do EVERYTHING together!

I'm so grateful for every experience I encountered, every storm I endured and every wrong path I went down. It was all necessary and part of God's plan for my life. I now understand why I had to go through what I went through. There are some storms we face that are not always necessarily for us. Sometimes, God allows us to go through things to show others that, yes you may be down and out now, but you can make it through. There are even times now, where I start crying and thank God for keeping His hands on me. HE GETS   ALL THE GLORY! I don't have to paint a false image anymore to impress people, stress about where I'm sleeping, what I'm eating, or how I'm going to pay bills. After my pain, God blessed me abundantly.

I don't care where you are in life right now or what storm you may be facing, know that it is going to work out for your good. Your pain isn't happening to you; it's happening for you. It's NECESSARY for where God is taking you. Through all of your tears, all of your losses, all of your mistakes, hold on to your faith in God. Even if you don't see how things will turn around in your favor, God does! You are going to make it past your pain.TRUST HIM, and know that after the pain…….it definitely gets greater.

STAY CONNECTED

Promise Brackens
pomisebrackens@gmail.com

THEN AND NOW

Jeanette Sewell

SAD
AFRAID
LOST
LOW SELF-ESTEEM

Those were the labels I wore for the majority of my life. At the age of six, I was molested, and it continued until I was thirteen. This set off a chain reaction in my life. I began to be very disobedient to my mother. Since my abuser was a man, I would think I would have hatred toward men. Instead of running away from men, I ran to men. I became very promiscuous. I thought this was what I should be doing. Besides, all I had ever known was men. To add to my agony, in March of 1988, at the age of fourteen, I lost my mom to domestic violence. That same evening in March, I learned that I was pregnant. Here I was motherless and getting ready to become a mother. I was devastated, heartbroken, and lost. I became a statistic, a "teenage mom" and an orphan. My mom was my everything. She was the only parent I knew. I grew up in a single-parent home.

My future wasn't looking good at all. I had my son and tried to be the best mother I knew how to be.   I met my ex-husband right before my sixteenth birthday, and he told me all the things I wanted to hear. There's a difference between what we want and what we need. By this time, I was two grades behind in school due to my birthday and my pregnancy. Then, I eventually dropped out of school. Now, I was a two-time statistic-teenage mom and high school dropout. Life as I knew it was over for me. My life continued to spiral out of control. My husband at the time had no idea what demons I was dealing with. I had no idea what demons I was dealing with. I never told anyone that I had been molested repeatedly. Who was I going to tell? This type of thing was not something you talked about. My demons got the best of me, and I needed help badly, but the question is, "Where do I go for help?" My ex-husband became very abusive. I guess he thought he could beat the demons out of me. My self-esteem was low. I had a child, I was a high school dropout, and I was going through mental and physical abuse. How was I supposed to feel good about myself?

    At the age of eighteen, I had another child. I also got my GED from Mississippi Valley State University. I passed the teacher's assistant exam. I felt that finally something was going right in my life for once. I applied for job openings in the school system, but I did not have any college hours, so I did not get the position. I became a welfare recipient to take care of these tiny little human beings that God had blessed me with. In 1996, baby number three came, and in 1999, baby number four followed. My relationship with my ex-husband did not get any better. I was told repeatedly that no one would want me with all these kids. He repeatedly told me that I didn't have anywhere else to go. He told me that he was my only hope. When you constantly hear these things, you begin to believe them, especially when it seems as if things are steadily going downhill for you. Between the mental and physical abuse on his part and the adultery on both of our parts, I grew tired of being on this rollercoaster ride with him. One minute we were up and the next minute we were down. At this point, I still had not gotten any help for the demons that were controlling my body. I was on a rollercoaster ride in my marriage. I was trying to figure out when it was going to come to a full stop. Sixteen years in, I figured out I had to be the one to stop this toxic cycle and get out, and I did. May 24, 2006, we divorced. I had taken care of one problem, but I still had to deal with the other problem. Were the demons still controlling me? Yes! Where could I get help for this addiction?

Three days before my divorce, May 21, 2006, I was working at Fred's Dollar Store. Several men walked in with accents. I automatically assumed they were from Africa. One of them replied in a sarcastic manner, "Do we look like we're from Africa? No, we are from Jamaica." The one who had gotten sarcastic continued to stare at me. It was obvious that there was a connection there. It was disclosed that they were in the United States working. Before leaving the store, the "sarcastic one" asked if he could have my number, and asked if he could possibly come back to talk to me after work. I gave him my number and told him yes. After my shift ended, we talked and that's when I discovered his age. I learned that he was 10 years younger than me. I was in disbelief. Thank God I didn't let his age deter us from building a friendship.

Jeremiah 29:11 says, For I know the thoughts that I think toward you, saith the Lord, thoughts of peace, and not of evil, to give you hope and a future." See, God knew the plans He had for me. Even though this man was 10 years younger than me, he was destined to be in my life. After building a friendship and after my divorce was final, he asked me if he could be my boyfriend. Of course, I said, "Yes." What did I have to lose? After being in an abusive marriage for years, even his friendship was refreshing. He took me on dates. I mean REAL dates. He showered me with his love. After three months of dating, he decided that he would not return to Jamaica. This was the turning point in my life. It was the beginning of something real. I couldn't mess this up with him. I didn't want the demons I dealt with in the past to interfere with the promises of God. After six months of dating, on November 18th, I said, "I do" to my Boaz. We attended church every Sunday and rededicated our lives back to Christ as one. It was something about this man that made me want him and only him. I know what it was- the God in him, the love, the compassion, and the stability he provided. Daily, I asked God to help me be a better wife to him than I had been to my ex-husband. God never let me down. I am proof that God will keep you if you want to be kept. The demons of the past no longer dominated me.

  I have no doubt that God sent this man to Fred's Dollar Store that Sunday evening. He was my promise after the rain. He motivated me to return to college to complete my degree from Mississippi Valley State University in Early Childhood Education. I had God in my life, a loving husband, my children, and a college degree. This was the chain reaction that I so longed for. I've learned over the years that our timing is not God's timing. Ecclesiastes 3:1 says, "To Every thing there is a season, and a time to every purpose under Heaven." When my Boaz came into my life, it was my season and my time. I am a living witness that God will deliver you. I can honestly say that I've been faithful to my Boaz for 14 years. God has truly been keeping me. My past is my past, and it will not be a part of my future. I don't walk with my head held low anymore. I know Who I am and Whose I am. The labels that were once placed on me have faded into the background.

JEANETTE NOW
RESTORED
BRAVE
SAVED BY GOD

STAY CONNECTED

Jeanette Sewell
jeanettesewell1002@gmail.com

Peaches Smith

At the age of fifteen, I lost my virginity to a young man whom I admired from the moment I entered high school. I thought he was so handsome. I wrote him letters every day, and I would wait at the stop sign on the corner until he came from baseball practice to give them to him. I was so in love with him even though he only liked me, I had created a relationship for us in my head

As time passed, I realized that he wasn't for me, and one specific night, he did something that crushed my soul, and it broke my heart. From that point forward, I put a label on all men- DOGS! I stopped talking to him, and began talking to other boys. I had in my mind that I can do what I want just like the boys. I had several that I was conversing with, and it did not bother me one bit because I felt as if I was getting my revenge.

So many things happened during this time, and I did so many things that I eventually earned a terrible name for myself. I did not care. As long as I was getting the attention that I craved, then nothing else mattered. I didn't care that they talked about me or laughed at me when I walked by because in my mind, I was the center of attention even if it was bad attention. I received so much attention that it started to control my life. I started to sneak out of the house. Every time my mother left for work, I left.

I did it up until she called me crying one night thinking I had run away, and she begged me to come home.

Shortly after that incident, I calmed down and realized that my mom was important to me, and I couldn't keep hurting her. I respected her guidance and stopped desiring to be the center of attention, until I met a guy who I felt was different. When we first met, I immediately felt that he was nothing like the "boys" in my past. He gave me butterflies and made me smile constantly. We began to date, he met my mom, I met his mom, and he would visit me at my house a lot. I was in love all over again. He was the only one that had my attention. I thought the feelings were mutual.

At some point during our courtship my family lost our home to a fire. He helped me through this very difficult time, and I was grateful. I guess I was so grateful that I allowed him to talk me into having unprotected sex, even though I wasn't on any kind of birth control. Of course, I became pregnant. I was so scared that I took three pregnancy tests just to make sure. He was so happy at first because this was his first child, but as time passed that changed. I went to doctor's appointments alone, I was very emotional, and I cried many nights. During my pregnancy, he walked to my house in the rain and ended our relationship. That broke my heart. I was pregnant and alone.

As time passed and the time approached for me to have our baby, he had almost stopped all communication with me. He would call from time to time, but it would only result in arguments that included him demeaning and degrading me. I eventually went into the hospital to have the baby. I begged for him to come and see our son and sign the birth certificate, but he never came. I must admit I was depressed after I had my son, and most of the days I sat in my room and cried for hours because I loved my son's father, and he abandoned us. He didn't even give us a chance. I wasn't eating or sleeping, and some days I didn't even want to hold my son. One day, my mom came into my room and said, "You need to come out of here. You have a beautiful son who needs you." I didn't think of it that way. I was so caught up in my emotions that I forgot about my son. At that moment, I realized that if his dad was there or not, I had to handle my responsibilities.

Today, I am 29 and my son is 11. He shows me love everyday, and he reminds me that I am a good mother without his father. Also, I recently adopted my daughter who is 11 as well. I want to remind every woman who is reading this to stay strong and fight. I want you to remember that women are built to be strong and withstand any circumstances that life throws at us. After my son's father left abruptly, I was lonely and depressed, and I had forgotten I had a reason to live. I do not ever want to get back to that place again. I did not write this for anyone to give me sympathy, this was written for empowerment. I wrote this because I overcame the depression, I overcame the loneliness, and I overcame the feeling of not being wanted. My best advice is to seek God first. We often put God last, and because of that, we don't get the best results.

I am a Powerful Woman of God now, and I can move any mountain that is in my way, and I encourage every woman to do the same. I will end with my favorite scripture: "The race is not to the swift, nor the battle to the strong, nor bread to the wise, nor riches to men of understanding, nor favor to men of skill. But time and chance happen to them all. (Ecclesiastes 9:11). Ladies, let us not forget that we are fearfully and wonderfully made and remember anything is possible with much perseverance and prayer. Do not give up on your dreams, even when life throws curve balls or when people turn their backs on you. Everything happens for a reason, and good things fall apart so better things can come together.

STAY CONNECTED

Peaches Smith
peachessmith966@yahoo.com

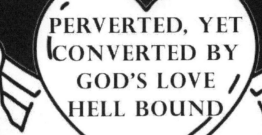

Every Sunday through Saturday, you could find me at my local assembly-worshipping, choir rehearsal, prayer service, and volunteering. I grew up being taught that church was life, and Jesus was the only way. (Side note: I still believe that, but there must be BALANCE.)

It was not until I was almost a high school graduate that I had my first movie theater experience. Imagine being in high school and escorted by a family member to the cinema. Embarrassing, right? I can remember not being able to have a boyfriend. Anytime a boy would call the house phone, you can almost bet my mom was on the other line listening. Due to an extremely strict home life, I began to read and write. I would always order books from the Time Life Book Club. Lord have mercy, I probably still have a balance with them. I did not just order any type of books. They had to be Arabesque Romance novels. These novels led me to journaling, writing scenes as if I lived the life of the authors that I was reading. What I did not know was those books, as well as other life choices would open me up to a life of pornography, promiscuity, and homosexuality.

High school for me was boring. I wore skirts all the time and only really hung out with a few people. Boys tried to talk to me, but the way my mother was set up, she needed to know your entire family lineage to approve of you even stopping by. There were only a few that mommy approved of. When the mandatory pants ban was lifted in the house, I began to hang more with the fellas. Hanging with the guys really pushed me to want to be one. I saw the way they handled the girls. I saw how they had more than one. I saw how the girls would come right back as if nothing happened when they cheated. I found that concept interesting early in life. Those situations prompted me to never want to be "that girl" in my life. However, it drove me to know that I could have "that girl" if I wanted to.

College was the life! I was finally free.

"No more shackles, no more chains, no more bondage, I am FREE!"

I was no longer under strict rules and it was time to WILD OUT or so I thought. Being in a new city and new state, I was terrified. I remember sitting in my dorm room, with the doors open, singing. It was during those moments of worship that I became tempted. *Can I just insert right here that the enemy knows what you like? * There were a group of ladies who stopped by the room to give me accolades on my voice. Appreciative of their comments, I kept singing. One young lady ended up returning to invite me to the club, which turned out to be the gay club. You see, I declined the first, second and the third time. However, this group just would not let up. *When the enemy is after you, he will try every avenue to get to you.* The gay club was an experience. I had never in my life experienced so many lights, flamboyance, and a space where it was cool to be you. It was almost as if I belonged. (Fact: It's dangerous going into unfamiliar territory not knowing who you are.)

This club led me to dancing downtown every Thursday, which was Ladies Night at one of the hottest mixed clubs. The bouncers and the DJ knew me by name.

Although I did not get paid to dance at this club, I brought a lot of entertainment to the business. You could catch me entertaining by dancing in the cage and on the speakers. I was not a stripper yet, but I sure felt like one.

*One sin opened the portal for more (James 1:14-16). It led me down a fallen path. Willfully sinning opened the door to be tempted even more. *

Dancing and homosexuality became my drug. One hit simply was not enough. My life became the breeding ground for the devil to have his way. I remember wanting to take my seductive dancing skills to the next level. I sought out strip clubs in the area, I was specifically looking for a classy club- much like myself. Failing to find one that fit my standards, I decided to go into business alone-private dancing. My mother never had to send me money anymore, but I was doing very well. I had my own place, a car, money, women, and men. The fast, flashy life was what I thought I deserved. I had completely strayed so far from God and my upbringing. If God had called while I was doing my own thing, I was HELL BOUND!

Still wanting to please my family, but not being delivered from my other demons, I ended up married and pregnant. While in that relationship, I denied that any of my past dealings influenced me. I tried to throw myself one hundred percent within the marriage. Yet, those demons that I dealt with as a young, single woman crept into my marriage. I even tried introducing my husband to the entanglements, so I would not feel bad about stepping out.

In my mind, I wanted to be delivered, but I was not strong enough to shake the enemy's temptations within my own strength. It was like I was living a double life- married, happy, church going woman by day and harlot by night. I even looked down on others whose sin was so dreadfully exposed. I mean, how could they not be discreet?

Tacky!

God was NOT pleased with me! My heart was dirty and unclean. He placed so much inside of me and I knew it. Yet, I willfully sinned. (Hebrews 10:26- If we willfully sin after we have received the knowledge of truth, there will be no more sacrifices.)

Then God had to BREAK ME piece by piece.

I was accused of child neglect and taken to court in an attempt to lose custody of my children. If there were ever a time I cried out to the Lord, it was then. I cried for days at the audacity of someone to even verbalize neglect. I lost weight, hair, my mind, and almost my children due to this lie. My marriage had deteriorated; I was numb. After counseling, divorce was the only option. I was hurt by how physically abusive the marriage had become and broken that my children would not grow up in a two-parent home. I even became suicidal because I had to face everything that transpired. I vowed to never love another man again.

I found myself falling back into that familiar place. As I reflect over my life, when things did not go my way, I always seemed to fall back to the familiar place. It was in the familiar place where I had control. It was in that familiar place where I could do what I wanted to do. It was in my familiar place where Hell was calling my name. It was not that I could not see past the hurt, I did not want to see past the hurt. I began blaming every man for my trauma. Truth was-I needed deliverance and I needed it FAST. The place where I worshipped was so caught up in my singing abilities that no one dealt with my demons. I was singing until people danced and shouted down the aisles, yet singing my way to HELL and no one seemed to care or notice.

Then one night, I had a real experience with Jesus. I began to think about the life I was living. I thought about how he had spared my life so many times. From the drug dealers to dancing for women/men, late night creeps to near death experiences, and almost losing my children, I just began to weep. I began to cry out JESUS......JESUS.... JESUS...Save me Lord!

Despite how awful I had been to God, He was good to me. He loved me so much when I was unlovable. There were times when I denounced serving Him. He never turned His back on me. When I took Him for granted, He still called me. When I mistreated others, He forgave me. When I contemplated suicide, He literally pulled me up from the dark place.The God that I served casted my sins into the Sea of Forgetfulness- never to remember them again (Micah 7:19).

Question? Who would not serve a God like this? I have seen God perform miracles and turn situations around on my behalf. Did I think I deserved it? No! However, his love covers a multitude of sin (1 Peter 4:8). I know that he can do it for you too. There is absolutely nothing my God cannot do. God converted my perverted heart and transformed me into a woman after His heart.

(Acts 13:22)

And when He (God) had removed him (Saul), He raised up for them David as king, to whom also He gave testimony and said, "I have found David the son of Jesse, a man after MY own heart, who will do all My will."

STAY CONNECTED

Alicia Nixon-Perry
Aj8433a@gmail.com

MASK OFF, FINALLY

Sherry Kinner

No matter what I had gone through or was going through at the moment, when I was around others, I was always bubbly and energetic Sherry. There was no way I was letting people know that my life was not perfect. I kept a smile on my face and partied as if I had just hit the lottery.

Then, as time progressed, life made it impossible to wear that smile. I stopped wearing a smile and adopted a "mean mug" to be portrayed as this "mean, nonchalant, stuck up" person when in reality, I am the total opposite. Because I have been hurt more times than I can count, in my mind, "the mean mug" helps me to hide behind the wall I built.

As a child, you see everything as innocent and harmless. That's how I saw the individuals that often visited my mom's house. At a very young age, I found that to be very untrue. First, a family friend began molesting me, and then family members followed suit. This went on for a while, and nobody noticed it. I was so scared to speak up, so I never spoke about it until I became an adult and began therapy. Even after speaking to my therapist, I still only had the courage to tell my then boyfriend who is now my ex and the father to my two deceased babies. Here I was, barely an adult. My first major loss was my innocence, and then at only 10 years of age, I lost the first man I ever loved- my father. Now, two children. How much more can I take?

That's not even half of the hurt I have experienced. I've taken many losses and each one seems to be more unbearable than the other one. I've lost a total of six children and with each pregnancy, the doctors always hoped that they had "the fix" to get me to carry for the full term. Each time they were wrong, and each time, my heart crushed a little more. Through each loss, a wall was built to toughen my external layer. I needed to protect myself from being hurt by others and life, but found that wasn't so easy after all. I pretended to be tough, but the truth is, I often felt very weak.

That weakness forced me into several failed relationships. I longed for my father, so I dated with the intent of finding a father figure, but I quickly learned that no one could amount to my father. I was looking for something that did not exist. After I let go of false hope, I finally found a man who I didn't see as a father figure and surprisingly, I fell in love with him.   He treated me well and for years, we both thought we had found "The One," but honestly, he wasn't ready for the next step. I began feeling like I wasn't enough to be his wife or maybe it was because I felt like I couldn't give him the children that he would want. We soon decided that we were better off apart, even though it wasn't really mutual. Being in that relationship for seven long years and suddenly being alone, I began to date myself. Then, a knock on my door would shake things up.

The man behind that door was a handsome, dimple-faced chocolate man with an infectious smile. He was there to install my internet and while there, we talked and flirted a lot. We soon learned that we had a lot in common and great chemistry after we began dating. We dated for a while and in December of 2019, we decided to make it official. The happiness this relationship adds to my life is amazing. We're not perfect, but we work well together. He compliments me multiple times a day, he opens doors for me, walks on the outside when we're on the street, and truly embraces holding my hand. The best thing in all of this is he comes with children- my bonus babies.

Even though I haven't decided to give pregnancy another try, I know that there's still hope and blessings in all of this. God has blessed me with a man who has children, and their mom willingly allows me to be in their lives. With all of those losses I've taken, I have finally been able to take the "mean mug" off and tear down the wall I've built.   I am free from all of that hurt, and I am free to truly enjoy life without having to wear a mask.

STAY CONNECTED

Sherry Kinner
sherry.kinner@yahoo.com

How many of us have looked at another woman and wished we had her attributes? We wish we had her smile, her figure, her intelligence, her wit, her house, her husband, her whole life. I'm sure we've all desired some element of someone else's life, especially when we don't know how they acquired these things or accomplishments. You see, there are those who perhaps see me as a young woman who has it all. There are some who see me and because we grew up together, they may assume they know me and all that there is to know about me. Well, I'm here to tell you that there's a story behind the GLORY.

Growing up in a small town has its advantages and disadvantages. One of the advantages is everyone knows you, and one of the disadvantages is everyone knows you. As humorous as it may be, it holds some truth. As a child, I learned very early on that there were things that I couldn't say, things I couldn't do, things I couldn't wear, and things I couldn't be because of who knew me or because of who I was. By the time I was born, my parents had gone through the early struggles of building a family and a business. By the time I was born they were beginning to settle into the benefits of their labor and commitment to Christ. So yes, as a child I didn't want for anything. I wasn't born with a silver spoon in my mouth, but it was definitely stainless steel.

Because of my particular upbringing in the Holiness church, I learned early on that righteous living was everything. Whether or not it was an intended lesson that was taught, I also learned that the perception of living a righteous life was to be treasured even more. With that being said, I learned to suffer in silence. Even as a child when things happened to me that would eventually shape my personality, my ideas about beauty, and my experiences with sex, I learned that as long as I continued to be a "good girl" that everything would be alright.

I've always been a "good girl." I had old-school parents who weren't having it any other way, and I thank them for that because it helped me in so many ways. However, it still had its caveats. One major caveat was it gave me a fear of disappointing them. It gave me a fear of tarnishing our family image, so when I was molested at the age of 5 by a close family member, I didn't tell my parents because I didn't want to get into trouble. I didn't want the predator to get in trouble. You see, I was a "good girl." Bad things don't happen to "good girls," right?

As a result of me internalizing that assault against my innocence, I developed severe anxiety attacks that manifested within the next year. By the time I was in the first grade, my anxiety attacks were so severe that whenever it was reading time, I vomited profusely everyday for about three months. It's amazing that now as an adult, I can see the dots, and I'm just now making the connections. Even as a child, I understood that putting on a brave face and being a good girl was what was best, right? I couldn't have been more wrong.

The anxiety attacks subsided after some time as a result of my parents addressing my verbally and mentally abusive teacher. You see, she was a battered wife who then came to work and batter us little ones. So there I was, a 6 year-old, juggling abuse and not yet having the voice to tell anyone to stop. I didn't have the understanding or articulation yet to reveal to my parents what was going on. Sure, their discernment revealed to a degree and they intervened when and where they could, but they couldn't protect me from everything.

The same predator who molested me would taunt me about my big nose. I had older male cousins who told me I was ugly. There was even an older male family friend that always called me "little boy" because I had a heavy, raspy voice for a little girl. Now enters compounding interest on an already thriving bed of anxiety and depression. I became depressed as a little girl because even though I was a "good girl," I was an ugly little girl.

Fast forward through many life experiences and exchanges, my anxiety and depression were such a part of who I was that I suffered in silence and many times contemplated suicide. Once in junior high, I tried. I took a handful of pills and chased it with cough medicine hoping to wake up dead. Well, I'm still here! God didn't allow me to die.

The point of me sharing these things is because there are those who have ALWAYS assumed because I excelled in academics at school, because I didn't misbehave and because I came from a good family that I didn't "go through" anything. People look at me and assume that the life I have now came undeservedly. If you only knew. If you only knew that had it not been for those things that happened to me, I wouldn't have developed a sensitivity to those who have been sexually and emotionally abused. Should those things have happened to me? No, but I'm learning that God doesn't waste our suffering. I'm learning that while I wanted to die from some of the experiences I've had in my life, God didn't let them kill me. Catch that!

Those things happened to me and God is using those things, as tragic as they were, and as tragic as some things still are, to develop me into a warrior.

Some of my experiences, though excruciating, were NECESSARY! It was necessary that I survived. It was necessary that I lived to tell my story now. It was necessary that I treasured being a "good girl" because it kept me from making so many foolish decisions. It was necessary that I developed a prayer life to combat depression and anxiety. It was necessary that I learned not to date men who verbally assault and belittle women. It was necessary that I was brought up in a sanctified church where I learned the power of prayer, and I learned that my praise was my weapon. It was necessary that I live. I've tried several more times to commit suicide, but God told me to live and not die and to declare the works of the Lord.

We all have a story behind the Glory. So, the next time you look at a woman and think she has it all, ask yourself first, "What did it cost her to be where she is? What does it cost to maintain who you see?" I'm not talking about makeup or material things. For every woman's smile, there were tears. For every healed scar, there were tears and blood shed. Let's kill the spirit of envy and jealousy towards one another because we really don't know what it takes to be any one of us. Let's handle one another with kindness and grace. See your sister for who she is and all she's gone through or is going through.

Regardless of what has happened to you or through you, remember it was necessary so God could mold you into the best version of yourself, and that's a woman who looks like Him.

STAY CONNECTED

April Watson
wats410@gmail.com

BETRAYED, BUT NOT BROKEN

Arieale Munson

Growing up feeling like the "black sheep" can leave you with feelings of emptiness. You long and look for acceptance from people and things that serve no purpose in your life.

I was that girl. You know how people show you who they are, but you still don't believe them? That's like touching a hot stove when you know you can be burned. When you have experienced blatant betrayal, domestic violence and emotional control-that alone builds up a wall, but that did the opposite for me. I used my test to become an advocate, author and activist. No, I'm not perfect. I'm still figuring out this thing called life, but I promise, I can show you what a living testimony looks like.

At 16 years old, I became a mother to a handsome young man. I had to come off the porch to the sidewalk to grow to become a young woman fast. Because I was told that no one would ever want a teenage mother, I put myself in situations that I knew that I didn't need to be in, such as abusive relationships. I had to take what I could get in life because who would want a teenage mother, right? That killed my spirit, but I honestly thought if I stayed in those relationships, that would mean that I was loyal, and that type of mindset kept me in abusive relationships.

After years of being put down, I decided that enough was enough. I was ready to spread my wings to get my life together, but I knew I had to tell the man I was dating first. I can remember that day, vividly. I asked him to meet me, so that I could tell him that the relationship was over; that conversation ended with me being knocked unconscious with a gun. I was found lying on the ground by my neighbor's house. We called the police to file a report, and after they left, he returned to our home and started shooting. This man was trying to take my life with my family inside as well. It was one of the scariest situations I had ever experienced. I knew when God allowed me to survive that situation, I had a purpose.

    I was a product of my environment. I allowed myself to be treated like I was nothing because I wanted to be loved. I didn't know myself. I knew God had a calling over my life, but I was running from my gift. Looking for something in different people, but getting the same results was my state of insanity. I was literally insane. How could I stay with someone who made me feel low, preyed on my pain and also used everything I told them against me?

    When it came to the people around me, I wanted everyone to win even if it meant losing myself. I did not care what sign I was shown, I was determined to make every situation work, and that sometimes caused me to be hurt myself. I had to learn that everyone doesn't have my best interest at heart. Because the people I thought loved me, turned out to be the ones who actually found every way to try to break me. Imagine trying to grow mentally, spiritually and financially, and the people who you think should be happy for you want you to fail. That's a tough pill to swallow. I was proof that a diamond in the rough can shine. That's when I realized my blessing isn't for everyone. God will take you the long route before he releases even a small glimpse of your future. He has heard conversations that you didn't, and he has gone in rooms before you. In my book, "When Pleasing Has No Purpose" I left no stone unturned for the deliverance of others who are bound in low life situations.

I want to inspire everyone to step out of captivity to gain their power back. To grow, we have to own our faults. A lot of times, we can't grow because we are still holding on to dead weight. No matter how God tries to pull us from a situation, somehow we find every reason to hold on. We can't do that anymore. In order for us to get over hurdles, we have to stop playing the victim in situations we've created. When we self-correct, it is a sign of growth. We don't have time to sit around drowning in our own misery because we only get one shot on earth. Everything that we experience, good or bad, is NECESSARY for our growth.

STAY CONNECTED

Arieale Munson
P.O. Box 41281
Memphis TN 38174
munsonarieale@icloud.com
www.arieamunson.com
901-677-3523

You can basically say that I was born with the odds against me. Black female child born to a teenage mother of two. My mother was forced to drop out of high school and my grandmother took on the responsibility of raising my sister and me. A lot of children deal with their fathers abandoning them, but growing up, all I wanted was my mom. You see, my grandmother was as mean as a rattlesnake and giving love wasn't actually her forte. On a good day, I might have been called a bitch a minimum of ten times. Although I had this huge hole in my heart where my mother belonged, she was still like a unicorn to me. She was this mystical beast who I loved, adored and yearned to see. Whenever I saw my mom, I was in awe of her beauty. Her smile was so radiant. She was so full of life. Her laughter would draw so much attention because it resembled a cackling scream. She always wore the latest fashions, and her hair was always done up so nicely. She always had stories about traveling and working at Disney World. My boring country life was no match for the things she had seen and done. I wanted to be just like her, but my grandmother was not having it. She tried over and over to destroy every good thought that I had about my mother, which I couldn't fully understand as a child. The truth is I saw the glitz and glam, but my grandmother knew the dysfunction.

I'll never forget the opportunities my sister and I had to visit my mom's home. I wish I still had the opportunity to live in the fairy tales because what I hoped to see and what I actually saw were completely different. I witnessed what my "mean as a rattlesnake, no love showing" grandmother tried to shield us from. I witnessed domestic violence and drug use too many times to count in my mother's presence. My dreams and imagination of who she was were shattered. The more I was around her, the more the radiance she once exuded diminished. By the time I was twelve, she became completely grey to me, void of all color and all shine. I grew up thinking that love was supposed to hurt because it was what I experienced. That and the fact that I never knew kisses and hugs or the words "I love you." So, I fell victim to my deep desires.

I was literally fourteen in an abusive relationship. Being hit almost everyday and called anything but my name, but for me that was love. A love so deep that I was willing to turn my back on any and everything just to have it. A love that would one day destroy my future marriage. It was during this relationship that I realized the realness of God. When I grew tired of being tormented, heart broken, beaten down, and stripped of everything positive about myself, all I found left WAS God. Sixteen years old and I wanted to die because I was so tired of being hurt, so tired of feeling the heartache and pain of loving someone who only loved money. I went from a straight A student, number one in my class, to being suspended and kicked out of school too many times to count, but I overcame it! God gave me the strength to move on, but pulling myself away from him was one of the darkest periods of my life.

I moved on and started putting the pieces back together only to find myself no longer a victim but the aggressor. I was heartless. I had no love or empathy for anyone or anything. I was running away from home, in and out of detention centers, literally living reckless. I had no respect for my mother who I eventually had to move with because my grandmother was critically ill. I can remember selling crack for my mom while she was out because she didn't want to miss a sale. If there was trouble, I was in it. My friends and I even started a female gang called the Lady Goons. I can remember a night where I literally robbed a guy while we were on the run and being sheltered by dope boys. Deep down, I knew that was not me. I was raised better than this. I was the little girl who went to church four nights out of a week and attended three Sunday services. I was lost, but God has a way of calling us home.

    The summer before I turned seventeen, I started dating an older guy. He was literally ten years my senior. Yet, he was the positive influence that I needed in my life. Of course, I lied about my age which was wrong, but things happen for a reason. I had plans to join the military in hopes of being able to financially support my older sister who was attending college in Washington, DC. I became pregnant and I just knew my life was over and thought I would just be another statistic. All of this occurred during my senior year of high school. It was at this moment that I realized that I was no longer a child and I couldn't make the same mistakes as my own mother. I started to fight to get better grades and to figure out what I wanted to do with my life. I fought my way up to number thirteen in my class and scored a 21 on the ACT to secure an opportunity to attend college. I gave birth to my daughter exactly eleven days before starting college. I was on my way to being a nurse and for the first time in my life, I felt like my family supported me. The cycle was presenting itself once again except in a different form. My grandmother reared my daughter for the five years that I dedicated to college. She didn't allow me to give up or drop out as she encouraged my mother to do, and for that I am eternally grateful.

I left the dream of pursuing nursing at MDCC and decided to become a teacher at Mississippi Valley State University. I was in for a rude awakening. In college, I found myself introduced to homosexuality, drug use, and the "old Jock" was back in full effect. My grandmother was busy raising my child while I was busy getting high everyday, all day. I would literally wake up to smoke sessions and end my day doing the same. I was a mess, literally.

I started to date other guys, even while I was in a relationship with my daughter's father. I remember being at a baseball game with one guy and connecting with another guy who would later be my husband. I was a player! However, I fell in love for the first time since I was fourteen. I am talking madly, deeply, dangerously in love. This wasn't me finessing a guy, this wasn't me liking him because his car was clean, this was love. I connected with this man and he brought me peace. The chemistry we shared was something you don't find everyday, it was very rare. Six months after meeting this man we were married. He had NOTHING! WE HAD NOTHING! All we had was love and each other. I struggled so much in that marriage and tasted so much of the bottom that I could look nowhere else but up. I gave birth to two children as an undergraduate in college. Although we were dead broke, God was still making a way out of no way. It was in this marriage that I found God. It was in this marriage that I learned how to truly pray and allow the Lord to order my steps. God filled me up until I overflowed, and I was the happiest I had ever been. I was having bible class inside of my home and being supported by women just like me. I was finally making my parents proud and developing a relationship with my mother.

The minute my marriage started to fall apart, I gave up on God. My faith was shattered. I started back smoking weed even with my husband while our marriage was in ruins. I was uncovering so much deceit and lies within our marriage that being high seemed to be the only thing that could ease the pain. I gained so much weight from smoking and eating that my husband no longer had a desire for me. My self-esteem was at zero. I can remember nights where I would cry myself to sleep because he wouldn't touch me. I was vulnerable.

This drove me back into the arms of my ex. I allowed my first love to come back into my life where he built up the woman he worked so hard to destroy years ago. The girl he made feel so ugly, he made her feel beautiful. The woman he picked apart, he put together. It was then that my husband attempted to fight for me, but it was too late. I gave up on my marriage and walked away after six years. I must have been out of my mind because I had invested so much in my marriage. I had just graduated college, moved into a new home, purchased new vehicles, and in the midst of all of the great things that were happening, I was tired. We remained together physically to preserve our business, but emotionally and mentally, we were finished. Though my ex had come back and built me up, truthfully I did not see a future with him as well because I was out of the realm of God. My friends started encouraging me to get out of my rut and just have fun, and I did just that. Focusing on me, my children and my career. I was free, and for the first time in my adult life, my life didn't include a man, and I was semi fine with that. The other part of me was hurting and devastated because I felt like a failure because my marriage had failed.

Months later, I met a man at work and at the time he seemed to be one of the most unattractive men I had ever seen in my life, but he was persistent. He messaged me every morning on facebook to tell me good morning and stopped by my job everyday just to get dissed. I eventually gave him a chance, and I eventually fell in love with who he was on the inside. I wish I could say that it was a happily ever after. I went through pure hell the first two years of that relationship, but God always has a way of finding his children when they are lost. I got my life back together with Christ and this man followed me. When I decided to be celibate, he supported my decision. This man wanted to be my husband. After a year of marriage counseling , we married. Though I did not see it in the beginning, he was God-sent. He pushed me in ways I cannot explain. Because of his support, I completed both a Masters and Specialist degree.

So much has changed in my life. I have an amazing husband and family. My marriage is healthy. My ex-husband and I have a healthy co-parenting relationship. I'm drug free! I am not abused! I don't cry myself to sleep at night! I have an amazing relationship with my mother. She is literally my best friend. I have a successful business! My husband no longer follows me to Christ, he LEADS me! Everything that I thought would beat me, shaped and molded me into who I am today. The abandonment, the abuse, the teenage pregnancy, the divorce, it led me here. IT WAS NECESSARY for my growth. It did not beat me!

STAY CONNECTED

Jockquelene Mitchell
jockqueleneward@gmail.com

JUST BREATHE

Jennifer Wilder

I can't breathe...
My heart is racing ...
My chest feels as if someone placed a ton of bricks on it and the weight is causing it to cave in.

My airway seems to be blocked, I gasp to try to capture even a micro breath, but I can't breathe.

If only I could move, but the strength that I once had has been depleted.

The warm tears are running down my face and chin and no matter what I attempt to do, there is no way to shut this leaking faucet off.

The pain is unexplainable, not just a simple cut or bruise, but instead it feels like the depth of my soul has been wounded.

If only I could have done more...

Maybe I should have noticed something before.

The thoughts haunt me daily, and my mind continually races like a hamster on a wheel.

I just want to breathe. Oh, God let me breathe, or at least let me smell his familiar cologne or hear his deep baritone voice. God give me anything to prove that this is not REAL. That this is just a NIGHTMARE.. but as I look over at the empty space beside me, I soon realize that this is my reality.

Take a Deep Breath ... breathe in ... Hold 5 seconds...Just Breathe

The day that you took your last breath was the day that I lost mine. It's been almost two years and these anxiety attacks seem to invade my normal day to day activities and life without any warnings or notifications. I've often been told that time heals all wounds, but that doesn't change my new title- Jennifer, the widow- that I am learning to embrace or the questions that I can't seem to find the answers to. Time doesn't bring back the memories that I've tried so hard to relive.

There are times that I have to write it down or say it aloud to prove that my happily ever after was not like the fairy tales that I read about as a little girl. I still remember as if it was yesterday- meeting the man of my dreams, planning this big extravagant wedding, and all of our long talks about the things that we were going to accomplish together. We had so many things left to do, but just like that- we ran out of time.

When I reflect on all the plans that I have made, I often laugh. So many things that I thought were going to happen or manifest, did not. We all do this daily-we make plans for our lives and even envision what our lives would be like, but what do you do when God has other plans? What do you do when God says NO? What do you do when the journey that life leads you on doesn't make sense? Well, I am a living witness to this. My life changed in the blink of an eye, and this change did not come with a manual or any type of instructions.

Isaiah 55:8-10 ~ " My plans aren't your plans, nor are your ways my ways says the Lord."

I remember it all so well. My husband called me while I was at work and requested that I leave and transport him to the hospital. This was definitely out of the ordinary because this man was one of the healthiest individuals I knew. However, since this was unusual, I proceeded with his request. Of course as I was driving I placed my doctor hat on and started thinking of all of the possibilities that could be causing him so much pain and discomfort. I thought maybe it was a hernia or some type of virus. After hours of tests, a team of doctors entered the room, and immediately I felt in my gut that something was really wrong. I could see the fear on their faces and I could hear the head physician's voice shake as he advised my husband and I that he had multiple masses in his colon and liver. I recall asking, "What kind of masses and what does this mean?" Although I asked these questions, I already knew the answers. Immediately my hearing stopped working and my voice became nothing but a whisper because I didn't know what to do or say. I wasn't prepared for this, and I did not know how to react to this type of news. He was young, and our lives were just beginning. We had two small children at home. What would this mean for them? I was speechless, but in my mind I had a million questions and as the doctors continued with their plan of action, I slowly stepped back, slumped down against the wall to keep from hitting the floor, and called on Jesus. I didn't have the strength to do or say anything else.

Psalm 46:1 God is our refuge and strength, an ever-present help in times of trouble

After he was released from the emergency room the following day, my life as I had known it turned into a whirlwind that I had no control over. There were numerous appointments, tests, and classes to prepare us for the biggest battle of our lives. Everything was moving so fast, and many days I didn't even know which day of the week it was. However, with each day, I prayed more than I've ever prayed in my life. I started each morning with prayer, I prayed while at work, in the bathroom, driving, I prayed and prayed. I became a prayer addict because I truly did not know what else to do. I knew that the load was too heavy, so I relied on God daily, and the word became my fuel and what I needed to get through the chemotherapy, medical trials, surgeries, and so many close calls that I lost count. Most importantly, I needed to be strong for my husband and children, who were both under the age of twelve. They had grown accustomed to sleeping in hospitals and spending many days trapped in a car traveling three hours away to doctor appointments. I worked 40 plus hours every week to ensure that my husband didn't feel the financial strain that was impacting us. I even took on painting jobs which turned my typical eight hours days to twelve to fifteen hour days, and these were the days I had to pray even harder. I found myself operating on pure adrenaline, and on many days sleep was just one of those vacations that I desired. I sacrificed so much, and I would do it all over again. Only God knows how exhausted I really was.

Four days before my husband's departure I had a dream of him getting out of bed looking like his old healthy self, his skin was glowing, and all of the bruises from being probed with needles were gone. I believe that at that moment, God was showing me that he was okay, or maybe God wanted to give me one last picture of the man I once knew. God is so good and so close to the broken-hearted that on the day that my husband died, He sent the Holy Spirit or maybe an angel to ensure that I would be okay with the chain of events that only he knew would occur. A young nurse who had been taking care of my husband came into the room at the end of her shift and asked, "What will you do if God doesn't heal him? What will you do when God says No?" I responded, " I will trust him anyway and let His will be done," and a few hours later I sat beside my husband's hospital bed and watched him take his last breath.

So, what do you do when God says no? You trust him anyway. You BREATHE! There are things and experiences that are NECESSARY, and we must go through them. Many of these times, you are left to experience things for your own personal growth, or there is someone else that we may meet who needs to hear our testimonies to survive or breathe. I personally have reflected on this journey of faith so many times and each time God has revealed something different, and trust me- He will give you beauty for ashes. I have been given the opportunity to share my story on many different platforms and in rooms I never thought I would enter. Though I did not understand why God allowed my husband to leave so soon, I trust God to be intentional and purposeful. Instead of being angry or bitter, I use my testimony to inspire others who have gone through or going through a similar journey. I am a host of a women's support group, a motivational speaker, and an author of a memoir that will be released early 2021 titled, "Just Breathe".

If you would like to walk through this journey of faith with me feel free to connect with me. My contact information is listed below.

STAY CONNECTED

Jennifer Wilder
Website : Jenniferwilderbooks.com
Instagram: The_authorjenniferwilder
Email:jenniferwilderbook@gmail.com
Facebook: JenniferWilder

BREAK FREE... SPEAK OUT!!!

Marisha Wallace

Growing up in my family, we really did not talk much about how we felt or discuss family issues that should have been addressed. This caused me to harbor feelings that built up resentment, bitterness, anger and rage.

I started being molested at a young age. My mom's husband started violating my siblings and me. This started when I was about four or five years old, and it continued until I was about nine years old. Finally, one of my siblings had the courage to speak out. However, the torture did not stop there. Because I was too afraid to tell that my mom's husband molested me, I would have to live with that secret for the rest of my life or at least until I had the courage to speak out about it.

To my surprise, my mom did believe my sibling who was brave enough to speak up about what was going on in our home, but she did not FIGHT for us. She removed us from the home, but she neglected to make him pay for the torture he caused us, and this left me with mixed emotions. When my mom left her husband, she left us too. It was like she blamed us for what happened to us. Shortly after, she started secretly using drugs, which oftentimes left us home alone to fend for ourselves. This caused my grandmother to raise us.

Not only was my mom not there, but my dad was not either. You would have thought that after my dad learned that we were being molested, he would have come to our defense, but that was not the case. So, there I was, left alone to figure out life on my own. When I entered middle school, I began fighting, getting suspended, and eventually was expelled from school. I even joined a community street gang to gain acceptance from my peers. My mom pretended not to understand what had all of a sudden gotten into me. Deep down I know she knew, but just did not want to face the truth.

I started having sex when I was fourteen years old, not because I wanted to, but because I thought that was what I had to do for boys to like me. I struggled with low self-esteem at an early age. I remember when the boys in my kindergarten class would pick on me and call me ugly names. I thought for boys to like me I had to do what they wanted me to do. That left me broken, lost, confused and struggling to find my identity. I had my first child when I was a senior in high school. Boy, was my mom mad, but how could she be? I felt that she did not do anything to prevent me from getting pregnant. She never talked to me about boys. She never told me to save myself for that special one. Everything I learned, I learned from either seeing it on tv or from my peers. After becoming pregnant, the father of my child decided that he no longer wanted to be with me nor did he want anything to do with the baby. Again, I was rejected and thrown by the wayside.

A year and a half later, I relived my childhood. A guy I met while working later became my offender, which left me pregnant AGAIN, lost, confused and with a bunch of questions. I went to my mom asking her what should I do in this situation and her exact words were, "You all need to come to a common ground for the sake of this baby because she will need you both in case anything happens." She was basically advising me to forget what happened and go on as if nothing ever happened, and that is exactly what I tried to do until I just could not take it anymore. This man would come around my family as if nothing ever happened. Every time I would mention what took place, my family would look at me in disbelief because "he did not seem like that guy." This man tortured me for months. This left me to deal with my emotions all alone and sent me into a state of depression. When I gave birth to my baby, I would not touch my baby or even want to be around my baby because of the thoughts from that night. Heartache after heartache, yet I walked around as if nothing was wrong. In all honesty I was dying on the inside, but that was only a surface of my pain.

In 2008, I met a young man who would only add to my abuse. Upon meeting him I knew from the beginning that I should have left immediately, but he told me everything I desired to hear from my parents. I went through five years of pure torture. He would cheat and I would be blamed for his cheating. He started physically abusing me because I would catch him cheating and he would take his anger and frustration out on me. I remember praying many nights for him to not kill me and for God to remove me from the situation. Many times God did, but I went back because it had become my familiarity. I thought that was the way a person showed someone he loved them. I thought it was okay as long as he apologized. I remember the night I was in the restroom cleaning myself up after yet another fight and contemplating killing myself because I thought that was my only way out. At that moment, God spoke to me. He told me, "I had a reason to live!" He told me that was NOT the plan that He had for my life and to trust Him. All that night I cried and cried and prayed and prayed until I could not pray anymore. I had mentally left the relationship years ago, but physically

I was still there hoping things would one day get better. Time and time again God showed me that He had better for me, but I could not see it because I was blinded by lust that I tried to fabricate as love.

It was not until I became pregnant with my last child that I decided that I had enough. That pregnancy was different for me, but in a great way. It was like God turned a light on, and I started to find my strength. I prayed and asked God to give me the strength to leave and NEVER look back. I stopped taking my problems to my friends and took them to the One who could give me a solution for it. After the birth of my baby, I started praying heavily asking God to get me out of that situation. I was VERY specific with everything I asked Him to do because I was finally done and wanted to not only give my children something different, but show them different as well. God provided a way of escape. Out of all my accomplishments, this was by far the best one yet. I left and started my journey to recovery. Many nights I longed to go back because he was familiar, but I remembered my promise to God. I started fasting day in and day out for strength because I needed God to step in and rewrite my story. When I started seeking Him, He started talking back to me, and that is when I accepted His call.

Looking back on the molestation, the rejection I faced from my parents, the rape, the acceptance I longed for and the abusive relationships- I count it all as joy. Yes, it happened to me, but it also happened for me. Through all that I endured, God was right there seeing me through it. Now I can tell young girls who may have experienced or are experiencing what I went through that there is still LIFE left in them, but it requires them to fight and let God see them through it.

My encouragement to everyone who will read this is-true acceptance comes from God. I now know what true love is because God took all of my broken pieces and created a masterpiece. When I look in the mirror, I see scars that I allowed God to heal. When I stopped adapting to the world's way of love and truly received His love, I was liberated. I now have peace. I now have joy because He saved me from myself. Love is NOT supposed to hurt. Instead of masking your pain, deal with your pain and let God put you back together! Stop holding on to what has happened to you. LET GO AND BE FREE.

STAY CONNECTED

Marisha Wallace
marishawallace11@gmail.com

I have been as lost as a ripple in the ocean.
 To the unkeen eye- seemingly going through the motions.
To a ship's captain- a hurricane forming, an emotional turmoil, set on fighting a ship.

I was only eighteen when I recognized the need for change in my life. Every part of me hated the life I was living. I lost my identity. Every day came and went seemingly more meaningless than the previous. The hobbies, the humor, and all things that made me who I was slowly evaporated. As a child and preteen, I had always been outgoing and noticeably confident. My childhood had been different from most, my parents had divorced when I was an infant. Co-parenting was a challenge because they lived in different countries. I became very close to my stepfather who passed away when I was only four years old. Shortly after, I moved with my biological father. He did his best at raising me; however, there were a lot of little things going on in my life that made me feel alone. Despite this, I still was able to keep an overall positive outlook on life, but the older I got the harder staying optimistic became.

I chose a group of friends in middle school, and we all started smoking marijuana. Eventually our friendship dissolved as we stepped into high school. I then found new friends who smoked marijuana as well. The substance became our foundation. It wasn't my intention to make many friends in high school because I started discovering how deceptive people could be. I felt betrayed by my loved ones and was more stand-offish. Because of my need to belong, how could I say no to being a part of the most popular clique in school? This clique left me unable to distinguish the good from the bad, choking with a hazed vision that left me silent, blinded, and lost. I started partying, and on several occasions, I passed out from drinking and stronger drugs than marijuana.

It saddens me now to think of myself in that situation, knowing how malicious and predatory men can be. Anything could have happened to me. For a while, I thought that was what life was all about. I was all about having a good time. I didn't have any direction or a life plan. I had accepted the fact that I wasn't planning on living much longer. At that point, that was not a suicidal thought. I just felt that the reckless life I was living would soon land me a trip to the morgue.

I knew that God would have to intervene if I wanted to live. The first step was recognizing that the life I was living had no direction. The drugs were at the wheel, headed for a death sentence, but I pleaded out. I turned to God and said, " I don't want the drugs, I don't want the friends, I don't want anything that doesn't serve me. I simply want to find myself." Nothing could prepare me for the way God was about to shake up my world.

When I prayed to find myself, I did. I found myself as I was- tied in a web of faithless relationships, quitting drugs then trying something stronger, relapse after relapse, and countless hospital visits and stays. They would treat the issue, but they did not connect me with a therapist which led to mental health issues. My mental health issues were hard for me to accept being that I was considered "gifted" as a child; it was even more difficult for my family to acknowledge it as well. We were in denial. We assumed it was just the drugs in my system causing my mental stability to quiver. The depression consumed me to the point that I was no longer able to deny it.

Suicidal thoughts moved into my mind for a longer stay. By then, I had attempted suicide several times, but I was unsuccessful. I felt as if my spirit had left my body. A crippling coldness took over me. We all know death is inevitable. It is at the end of each of our roads. Some people fear death while others glamorize it as pearly gates and an all-white party. For me, it was a craving. That's when I knew I had hit rock bottom. Living life with death as the objective is sure to bind you with the numbness and careless emotions that make the idea of dying so appetizing.

I am so grateful our pasts do not erase our future. I am so grateful that God gave me something to look forward to. I am so grateful He rescued me. It was not an easy journey, but with God, I started the road to healing, recovery, and a new life. I will admit that those same dark thoughts come and visit every now and then, but no longer do they defeat me because instead of me trying to fight for me, I allow God to fight for me. They visit less often when my focus is on God. That reassures me to keep my focus on Him and all will be well.

My encouragement to you is-mental health issues are very real and consuming, do not be embarrassed to ask for help. Seek help from where you see fit, whether it be spiritually or medically. It's important to stabilize yourself in order to love yourself. Maintain a healthy diet, do more of what you love, exercise to release emotions that you do not wish to harbour, stay up-to-date with issues concerning mental health, and keep your Faith in God.

When you struggle with believing in yourself, remind yourself that God believes. Always trust and believe that He has a plan for your life more solid than your own.

STAY CONNECTED

Estefania Suarez
aguirreori@gmail.com

The average sixteen-year old would be planning her SWEET 16, but here I was planning a baby shower. My childhood turned into motherhood within the blink of an eye. A baby was about to have a baby. I was nervous and an emotional wreck. I just knew my precious daughter would lack many things because I was lost. When she arrived, it was terrifying, but I gave her the best life a young, single, and jobless mother could. Just when I had gotten used to this "parenting thing," I learned that I was expecting AGAIN. Though I was two years older, I was still a child when baby number two made a grand entrance into the world. I beat myself up a lot for placing myself in the same situation again Things became rocky and postpartum depression began to strike. It seemed that I used pregnancy as a cure to my pain. I became pregnant again, but this time with twins. I went from two children to four children in what seemed like a blink of an eye. Then the unimaginable happened, one of the twins died just a day after birth. I was devastated. Though I felt that I was not ready to be a parent to four children, I wanted all my babies alive, well, and with me.

Losing my child took so much from me. I thought that was all of the pain I could bear, and then the unimaginable happened again. Three children became two after a house fire claimed the life of the other twin at only twenty-one months. I fell into a deep depression. As time progressed, I began to endure the pain a little better. I finally made it to a point where I could no longer see the flames or the fire. They were burned out, or so I thought.

The flames and fire decided to visit me once again. Imagine witnessing your mom burn in a fire and you can't do ANYTHING. Calling the ambulance even seemed hopeless. Over 65% of her body was covered in 2nd, 3rd, and 4th degree burns. Once my mom was admitted and stabilized, she was placed in a medically induced coma. Seeing my mom on the ventilator sent me into total shock. In my entire life, I had never seen my mom helpless as such and hospitalized to that extent. We spent the majority of her visiting hours with her, and when we were not there, the phone calls from the doctors and nurses caused me to panic. At any time, I thought the calls were to inform me that it was over. I can say that watching my mom fight gave me hope. My mom did not succumb to her injuries, and I never once heard her complain. She fought until she was released from the hospital. I often questioned God, "Why do bad things happen to good people?" Everything that was happening also put a strain on my children as well because they were seeing me at my worst. Depression and insomnia became great friends of mine until I was prescribed medicine. The medicine helped out a great deal, especially with sleep. Because I didn't want to become dependent upon them, I made the decision to stop.

My daughter was there to pick up right where I left off. After fourteen years of heartbreak and turmoil, she decided to attempt to end her life. My world turned upside down when she explained she had taken eight 600 mg Arthritis Tylenol and a few of my antidepressants. When she awakened to see that it hadn't worked, she consumed five more in hopes that the next time she'd succeed. BUT

GOD! She lived and was sent to a Mental Health and Behavioral Facility because she was now declared suicidal. Those seven days seemed like a lifetime. My daughter was all I could think about from the time I'd awake until the time I'd fall asleep. When I was notified of her release date, I couldn't get there fast enough. That reunion was one to remember. I don't think I've ever cried that much. I was overjoyed that I didn't have to face a mother's worst fear again- burying a child.

It seemed that death and near death experiences became the familiar for me. After losing two children and almost losing my daughter, I knew that God would not allow me to bear the pain of death anymore. However, I was wrong. I still remember the last conversation between my younger sister and I vividly. Her last words to me were, "I'll talk to you later." However, later never came. Unfortunately her life expired at the tender age of 13, just when we began to build a better bond. Because we were around each other more than ever before, it made the load of her death a lot heavier. There were so many things I had in store for our future together. The times we did share, I'll cherish forever. Of course, my faith in God slowly vanished. I was empty, broken, and confused and the weight of the world was heavy on me. The battle I was fighting seemed never ending. How could God love me and allow me to go through so much hurt?

As you can see, life can be REALLY hard. Some even call it unfair. I've since learned that we have to hurt to heal, and we must praise God in good and bad times. We tend to focus on the problem more than the solution. When we fully trust in God, we can not worry or try to fix it ourselves. He begins to fight for us. With whatever we face, He is always there to receive us with open arms and will never abandon us. God has infinite power and His love is unconditional. In the midst of my trials and hardships, I can truly say that I'm a living testament to His faithfulness. I pressed on through depression and so can you. "Don't give up on God, because He won't give up on You."

STAY CONNECTED

Felicia Lashawn Little
dnaisjah_0304@yahoo.com

Sometimes I ask myself, how am I still standing after being raised in Memphis, Tn. I was raised in Orange Mound where you saw and got a little taste of everything. I was introduced to dice games, gangs, drugs, strippers, doors getting kicked in, and everything that came with the streets very early in life. Then to add, I entered adulthood at an early age because I made an adult decision. I became pregnant at the age of fifteen, and this is when things became more real. I had to decide to either be the one who makes excuses or be the one to get things done. I put my big girl panties on and chose to get things done. Luckily, I did not have to do it completely alone. Having my great grandmother, my grandmother, my aunt, my mother, my uncle and my support system made it easier. Eventually, I dropped out of high school because I felt overwhelmed and became a victim of my circumstances. I beat myself up a lot for having my daughter early and felt as if I wasn't enough. Thoughts of suicide crept into my spirit, and the thought of letting my mom down weighed heavily on me.

Things started to shift and go downhill for me even more. My mom went to jail. I wrote and talked to her often, but that wasn't enough. I needed her with me. I felt so alone. I knew my father and spent time with him from time to time, but he was different, unlike my mom, so it was a different bond. Thank God my mom was not in jail for a long time. After she was released, we were a family again.

My mom decided that we needed a change of scenery, so we moved to a better part of the city. Now that I reflect, this was the best decision she could have ever made. I needed a new environment. I needed to see something different. Things started going well. I started my first job at Wendy's and with my earnings, I bought my first car. I enrolled my daughter in daycare, so I could take some pressure off my mom. Unexpectedly, I reconnected with my daughter's father which was amazing because daughters need their fathers. I wanted my daughter to have that bond with her father that I did not have.   In the process of us co-parenting, the unexpected happened; we fell deeply in love with each other, and eventually, gave birth to a second child. Although my children's father was the provider, and he ensured that we had everything we needed, I wanted better for my life.

After having my son, I set goals to make myself better for my children. I wanted to give them a better life than I had, and I understood that the change must first start with me. I wanted my daughter to look at me and desire to be just like me. I decided to get my GED; I passed the exam on the first try, and from there, it seemed that God started opening door after door. Fifteen years later, I thank God for keeping me because life is beautiful. Who would have ever thought that a high school dropout would be doing so well?   I now have a Bachelors and Masters Degree in Business Management, the owner of a custom T-shirt company, creator of Hustle No Handouts and Rich At Heart Clothing, and also the author of my first self-published book "No Handouts." The same little girl who suffered from suicidal thoughts and feeling worthless is now a beautiful woman who is excelling. Now, I am an example to my daughter of who she can become and an example of the type of woman my son should desire to marry. I am a testament that God never leaves us nor forsakes us. I am proof that our past does not erase our future.

I can admit I settled for some things, and it was because I thought I had to. I felt that after I dropped out of school and became a teenage mom, I was not worthy of great things. Now that I love me and know my worth, it is a beautiful feeling. I encourage women to get to know themselves and to love themselves, flaws and all. Know that you are beautiful, never settle, do not give up. "No matter what your past is, use that as fuel to go harder."
-Jamese

Follow your dreams and keep God first above all. If I can do it, you can, too. God is not done with us yet.

STAY CONNECTED

Jamese A. Greer
jamese_greer@yahoo.com
www.hustlenohandouts.com

DUMB
WORTHLESS
PATHETIC
PITIFUL
UGLY

Along with those labels, I was also told, "You're only going to be good enough to be someone's house maid." I started to believe those horrible things people said to me. I felt so worthless, and my self-esteem was at zero. How could it not? It had gotten to the point that I felt so ugly that I wouldn't even look at myself in the mirror. Along with this, my father died of cancer when I was fifteen years old. That following year, I engaged in sexual activites, and I craved sex to try to heal the emptiness I was feeling. I eventually became pregnant and became a mom at the age of sixteen. I didn't have a clue about what to do, but I did have help from family members. While trying to juggle school and be a mom at the same time, it was difficult. I wanted to give up badly. I was talked about for being a teen mom by my schoolmates, teachers, family members, and the community as well. I was so depressed, and I didnt know who or what to turn to. The depression caused suicidal thoughts to creep in, but I could not because I had a little person to care for, and those beautiful, bright eyes encouraged me to fight.

It was not long before the person I thought I was in love with turned on me as well. I was verbally abused daily, but I never could find the courage to leave. Though his actions clearly communicated that he did not love me, I loved him. After each episode, he would apologize and then I would let things slide. The cycle became repetitive. Then, I found myself pregnant again. How would I provide for these babies?

After I had my second child, I was talked about again. During the pregnancy with my second child, the fights with my boyfriend continued. The fights had gotten so bad that he choked me to the point that I could not breathe. I still stayed. He had given me disease after disease, but I still stayed. I thought this was love. Here I was a teenager, still trying to maintain school and care for two children. The cycle continued. By the time I was twenty-three, I had five children. I ended up on welfare, food stamps and government assistance. Everyone, including myself, viewed me as a young, dumb, little girl with a lot of children.

In the midst of dealing with being torn down from the outside, my boyfriend was tearing me down from the inside. One day, out of the blue, he decided he no longer wanted to be with me and his children anymore. This crushed my soul. How could he not want me anymore after all these children and after all we had been through? How could he just walk out of my life with all the history we had? That didn't matter. I didn't matter. Our kids didn't matter. Things continued to go downhill for me. Shortly after being forced to take care of my children on my own, I lost everything in a house fire. I remember crying out to God asking, "How much more can I take? How much more pain do I have to endure?" What I did not realize is that God was putting me in a position to need Him, and I am grateful He did.

It is when we are down to nothing that God is up to something. Sometimes God has to break up to make us. While I thought I was losing, God was putting me in a position to win. Yes, everything I endured hurt me, but it also helped me. So many people counted me out because I had five children by the age of twenty-three, but God was counting me in. Today, I am doing well and my children are well taken care of; because I depend on God, we lack nothing. I learned that while people may walk out on you, God will always be with you. Now, I am strong because I have been weak. God is my everything now. My faith is stronger than it has ever been. Through all my losses, I found me.

STAY CONNECTED

Tashika Williams
tashikaw19@gmail.com

I PLANNED MY FUNERAL

Natasha R. Knox

One day I woke up and decided it was over. I was sick of feeling and being defeated. I was tired of the pain and heartache that came in waves. Life would periodically hit me, then the depression would follow. I was vibrant and bubbly by day, and a mental case by night. I found so many reasons to get up in the morning, yet I couldn't find a single reason to rest at night. There was no way the God I served wanted me to live like that. So, I started rewriting the end of my story.

It was like any other Sunday morning-so quiet and still. I remember it well because I woke up scanning through the channels on my tv looking for a "feel good" show to change my mood. There was nothing on except televised church services and sad gospel music being played. I grabbed a legal notepad from the top of my closet, along with a pen and got comfortable in the middle of my bed. I remember a sad feeling overcoming me. I always thought I would have a great life, full of laughter, success and love. It was far from that, in my opinion.

It began. I started drafting and composing my own funeral. At least if I was going to change the end of my story, the least I could do was alleviate my family and friends from the pain of having to figure out what I would have wanted. First, I checked the face value of my life insurance policy (I hadn't even considered the fact that suicide would have also canceled any pay-out on my policy). Once I figured the amount of money my family could spend, I began looking for caskets online. This would give them a general idea of the style and the costs associated. I didn't want them to pay a ridiculous amount of money on "putting me away," so I chose a basic looking casket. I mean, they would only be able to see it a few hours, so it made sense to spend as little money as possible.

The next thing I did was include notes about where to purchase flowers, the location to use for the services, and where I wanted to be buried. I also included the names and addresses of close friends who my family didn't quite know. I left no stone unturned. I completed my entire obituary, INCLUDING the cover photo. My life was huge, so I chose a full color format, using full pages just to be sure everything fit. I wrote a beautiful autobiography, and outlined the order of the programme. I wasn't sure if the people I designated for certain parts of the service would be available, but I knew it wouldn't be that hard to find a substitute. My family would be so relieved to know everything was already done. From the selection of pallbearers and the location of the repast, I had completely planned my funeral. None of this scared me. It was time. My life had run its course, and I was simply existing in a world where I could no longer contribute anything to the lives around me. This became my mindset, and I was content with it.

The difficult part came. I never had a true plan of how I would end it all. I was so sad during this time- sad because I wanted to go, sad because of the people I would be leaving behind, and sad because of how sure I was about the entire process, but it needed to be done. My time was up, and there was no escaping everything I was battling in my mind. It was simply time. I started googling

"Peaceful ways to die." Google was so user friendly. It never asked "Why?" It never questioned my sanity, and it surely never tried to talk me out of it. After a few days of "searching," I finally came up with a solid plan. I chose to take an undisclosed amount of prescription pills, and go to sleep.

The actual day of my planned suicide came. I was so nervous, but I never felt unsure. I went about the day as normal. I ate whatever I wanted. I listened to music. I did everything that made me forget about how heavy the weight of the world was on my shoulders. The one thing I didn't do was call any of my family or friends. I didn't want to be "convinced" to stick around. Besides, I knew that reaching out to anyone would be considered "a cry for help"and I didn't want any help. I wanted to go.

As it got closer to bedtime, I followed my normal routine. I took a long, hot bath and curled in my freshly made bed. And then it happened. I gulped down every pill I had with a glass of water, and laid down for the last time. I asked God to heal the hearts of the people who loved me, and to forgive me for choosing my own expiration date.

"What have I done?!" I remember yelling as the pain awakened me out of my sleep. I began throwing up profusely. It felt like someone was tying knots in my stomach and tightening them. I was in so much pain that I had no choice but to seek medical help. This was not in the plan, and I knew the moment I decided to go to the hospital that I would survive. I didn't want to suffer, so I went. On the way to the hospital, I could barely see over the steering wheel because I had no other choice except to be slumped over due to the pain. Once I arrived, I was immediately taken back to observation. I remember total restoration by the time the doctor came in. It was as if nothing was wrong with me. An overwhelming sense of comfort had overcome me, and I couldn't explain it.

I explained to the nursing staff what I had done, and they began to follow protocol. They ran tests, and prepared me for a forty-eight hour stay in a psychiatric unit for assessments. Every single test they ran showed no signs or indication of an overdose. By this time, two things were certain. The medical staff was sure I was battling a mental diagnosis, and I was absolutely positive that God had His hands on me.

The next few days were spent in a special hospital where I received an abundance of love and assurance from the staff. To this day, it is by far the best thing that could have ever happened to me. In those days, I reconnected with God on a deeper level. I began to understand how trials are used to prepare us for our purpose. I spent so much time focusing on the forces against me that I forgot about the greater One who was always for me.

Everything in life has purpose. You see, I needed to kill me, so God could fulfill the will He has for my life. It was never what I anticipated, though. Yes, I planned my funeral but I never realized it was only for my flesh.

STAY CONNECTED

Natasha R. Knox
Lovelyhalle25@gmail.com

Dear God,

   Thank You for being an amazing God. We love You, and we are grateful that we are Yours. Forgive us for the sins we have committed against You. Renew the right spirit within us and set us on a firm foundation. We ask that You search us thoroughly, and if You find anything within us that makes it an uncomfortable dwelling place for You, remove it. Tune our ears to your voice and lead us into our purpose. Help us to see ourselves the way You see us- beautiful inside and out, whole, complete, & lacking nothing. Help us to understand that our pasts have no bearing on our futures, and regardless of where we have been and what we have done, You still love us, and it has not changed Your purpose for our lives. We decree and we declare that our best days are ahead of us…
…and it is so. In your darling Son, Jesus' name we pray, Amen.

Made in the USA
Middletown, DE
04 October 2020